Angels and Miracles

AN UPLIFTING COLORING BOOK

With Chicken Soup for the Soul Stories of Hope, Answered Prayers and Divine Intervention

Chicken Soup for the Soul: Angels and Miracles

Published by Chicken Soup for the Soul, LLC www.chickensoup.com
Copyright ©2023 by Chicken Soup for the Soul, LLC. All Rights Reserved.

The publisher gratefully acknowledges the many publishers and individuals who granted Chicken Soup for the Soul permission to reprint the cited material.

Cover and Interior by Daniel Zaccari

Printed in Canada

30 29 28 27 26 25 24 23   01 02 03 04 05 06 07 08 09

Saving Jordan

One thing you can say for guardian angels: they guard.
They give warning when danger approaches.
~Emily Hahn

Washing dishes has always been my pondering, preparing and praising time. The winter of 1987 was only different because washing dishes was not a choice, but an everyday reality in Kitzingen, Germany, where we did not have a dishwasher. Evenings tended to be very quiet after the boys were down because we were also television-less and basically radio-less since our apartment was out of signal range for the American AFN station, and I didn't speak German well enough to bother with the German stations.

This particular winter evening, I was looking out the window, washing the day's dishes and thinking about our life and how grateful I was for it. My husband, Jesse, was a U.S. Army tank company commander on maneuvers in the south, and his job allowed us to live in a beautiful village in Germany and gave me the privilege of staying home with our sons. Just that day, I had bundled up both boys in their winter gear, strapped them into the stroller, and rumbled over the cobblestones down to the village to buy our seasonal vegetables.

The ladies at the local greenhouse twittered over two-year-old Jacob and newborn Jordan. The ladies enjoyed spoiling the boys, teaching them German words just as I taught them English ones.

When we came back from our errands, I fed the boys their dinner and settled them down to sleep. Then I lowered the stack of plates into the hot sudsy water, figuring I would get the washing out of the way and then spend a cozy evening reading.

"Check the baby." It was just a fleeting thought, as I put plates in the drain board. I ignored it and started to wash the glasses.

"Check the baby!" This time, I felt it whispered in my ear.

Even though I knew that I was alone, I still turned around to see who had spoken. No one. A still small voice, easily brushed aside as imagination. I picked up the first glass, swishing the cloth inside to clean it.

"CHECK THE BABY!" Crash! I dropped the glass on the floor as the louder than audible voice thundered in my heart. There was no ignoring this messenger.

I ran into the nursery and turned on the light to find that six-week-old Jordan was still and blue. His chest was not rising and I couldn't feel any breath coming from his nose. I picked him up and checked his airway, then started infant CPR while running across the hall to my neighbor's apartment. Jordan took his first gasp as Anita opened her door.

When living in the United States, I knew that in a medical emergency to call 911. In Germany, I had no idea how to call for an ambulance. I knew that we needed to go to the hospital, but the fastest way to get there was to drive. While I drove, Anita kept watch over Jordan, prepared to start CPR again, as I raced through the cobblestoned villages to the American hospital in Würzburg. All the while, the same voice whispered, "Peace, peace, peace. I am with you."

That calming voice stayed with me during the whole time that we were at the hospital. We were one of the lucky families. Jordan was diagnosed a SIDS baby (Sudden Infant Death) but he survived and went on to play football, marry his high school sweetheart, serve his country in Afghanistan and Iraq, and graduate from law school. Through many instances in his life I continued to hear that voice whisper to me, "Peace, peace, peace. I love him more than you ever could." I always listen.

– Sharon Carpenter –

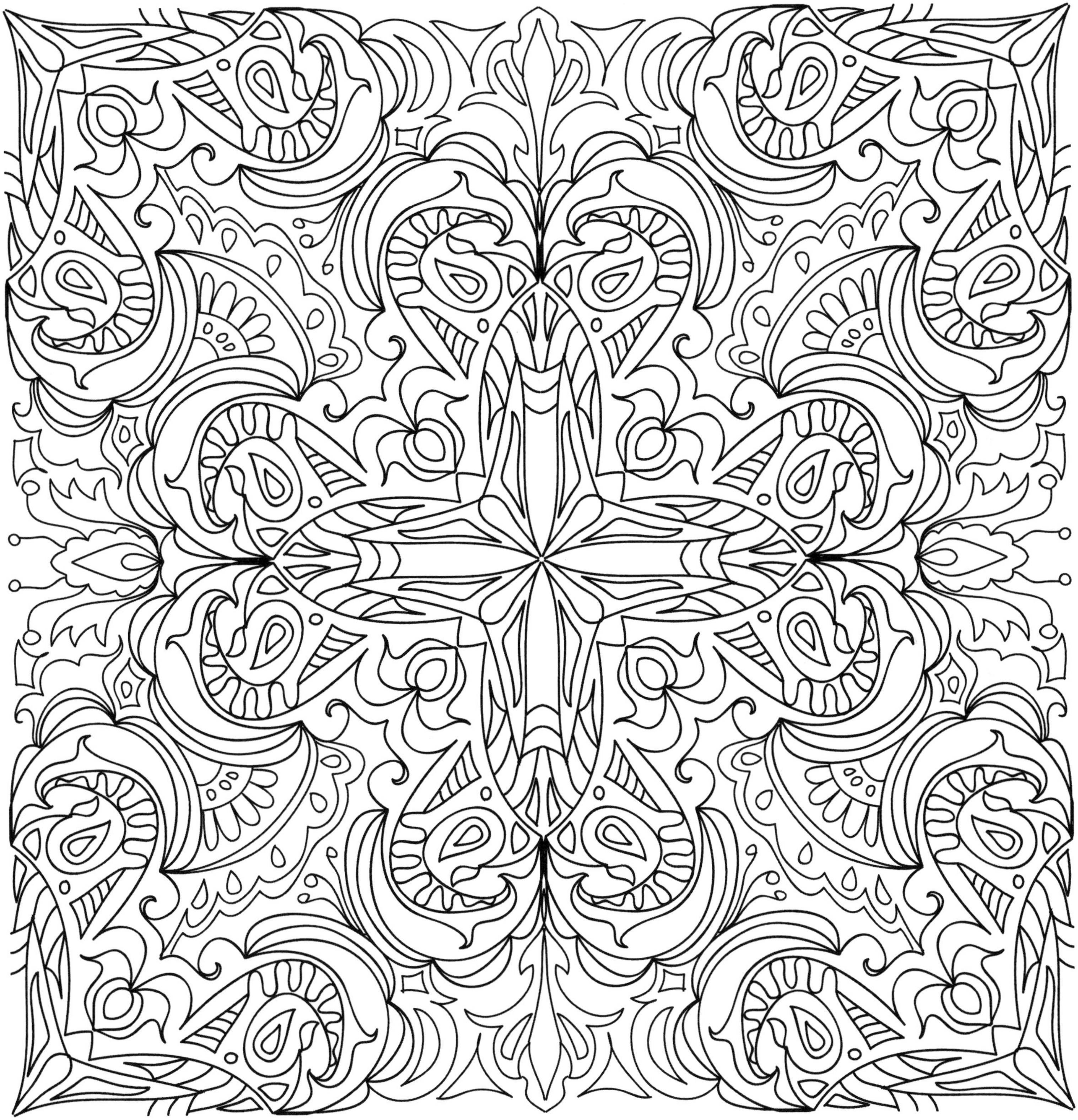

The Craigslist Vanity

The picture that accompanied the Craigslist ad showed a beat-up vanity in need of a major makeover. It was perfect! The seller, who lived nearly fifty miles away, even graciously offered to meet me halfway.

I found our meeting place, a local IHOP, and pulled in. I surveyed the parking lot. It didn't appear the lady I was meeting had arrived yet. I turned to check the back of my SUV and discovered I would need to do some major rearranging to accommodate my newest "Trash to Treasure" project. I opened all of the doors, and stacked some items to make room. Satisfied with the results I climbed back in my car. I took one last look in the rearview mirror and discovered I had not shut the back passenger door. I got out and walked around to close it.

There on the ground lay a single red silk rose that had fallen out of my car. I bent down to pick it up when I distinctly heard a voice in my head say the words, "Leave it there, it's going to mean something to someone." I stopped and looked around. I had come to trust that voice but I certainly didn't want someone to see me and think I was leaving my trash for someone else to clean up. I shrugged my shoulders, closed the door, and got back in my car, leaving the lonely rose in its place.

I couldn't see the far end of the parking lot from my vantage point. I decided I'd better make sure my fellow "Craigslister" wasn't waiting for me on the other side of the restaurant, so I put the car in reverse and pulled out of my space. No sooner had I started forward than a lady driving the truck I had been waiting for pulled in and waved at me. I took the spot next to her, only a few spaces down from where I had originally been parked.

She got out of her truck and introduced herself. She was a pleasant lady in her early sixties. As she helped me load the vanity into the back of my car I joked that my husband would be thrilled I was bringing him another project to complete. She laughed and shared that she had always done the same thing with her husband when he was alive. We got the vanity loaded and continued our small talk. She mentioned her husband several more times and the fact that she was a widow. She shared that she was having a hard time since her loss.

I understood about loss. My daughter had died in a car accident only a few years earlier. I asked her if she was familiar with the *Chicken Soup for the Soul* book series. She knew it well.

I told her about the book, *Chicken Soup for the Soul: Messages from Heaven,* explaining that after my own loss I found great comfort in its stories of people who had dreams and received signs from lost loved ones.

"Yes, I know exactly what you are talking about with signs!" she chimed in. She prepared to share her story when she stopped, suddenly transfixed on something behind me. She began pointing excitedly.

"Is that a rose?"

I turned around. She was pointing at the red rose that had fallen from my car.

She was excited and talked as if she couldn't get the words out fast enough. "I always tell my friends that the last time I received flowers was when my husband was alive. My husband was always bringing me bouquets of flowers and little coffee cups with floral arrangements in them. Anytime I see a flower lying somewhere I pick it up and I think of it as my sign from him that he's still near. I have an entire collection of flowers I've found since he died."

I looked at her in disbelief. I told her where the flower had come from and how I was going to pick it up but a voice told me to leave it because it was going to mean something to someone.

She got teary-eyed and asked if she could have the rose. I stepped to the side, making room for her to pass. "It's yours. I'm pretty sure it was meant for you," I told her.

She walked over and picked up the flower. When she faced me again, she was crying. We stood in the parking lot a while longer, two strangers sharing their hearts with one another. As we talked the woman twirled the red rose between her fingers while her hands shook with emotion.

I left the parking lot with more than a vanity that day. I left the encounter with a renewed sense of faith. Turns out that flower did just as much for me as it did for the lady for whom it was intended. And I just thought I was going to buy an old piece of furniture!

–Melissa Wootan–

As I sit here writing this I'm still amazed that just when I needed it, hope flew in on a hummingbird, solidifying my faith in things unseen.

Excerpt from "Hummingbirds from Heaven" by Amy Catlin Wozniak, a story in *Chicken Soup for the Soul: Angels & Miracles*

Heavenly Possible

I sat numbly with the occasional tear slipping down my cheek. I kept replaying the doctor's words: "I believe it is cancerous, although it seems to be a strain I have not seen before."

The tumors were on my tongue, and part of it would have to be removed. I was told it would severely impede my speaking ability and there would be little to no chance of singing again. This was devastating to a pastor and a singer.

I couldn't remember a time in my life when I had not been singing. My first solo was at age three. I never had any training, but I let my heart guide my voice and they seemed to make a good team.

I had joined the church to sing in the local Christian choir as a young girl. After that, I joined worship teams, Christian bands, appeared in musicals and even went on mission trips which focused on spreading the news via song. Now my songs would be silenced forever. How could God use me if I was silenced?

I had the surgery and went through two painful months of recovery. And then tumors returned. I went to another doctor, and had more surgery and lost more of my tongue. Now there was no chance of singing and even speaking would be difficult.

I remember speaking to a dear friend before the surgery, asking her what I should do. Deb, in all her wisdom, said, "Be the first."

"What?"

She reminded me of the struggles I had overcome my entire life. I had already survived two other kinds of cancer. She told me I was strong and that I needed to be the first to do what the doctors said couldn't be done. Be the first to speak well. Be the first to sing. Just trust God, believe in myself and do it!

Upon waking after surgery, I had a nurse approach me, laughing. She said that before I went completely under the anesthesia someone had commented on the size of my breathing tube. They were worried about it scarring my throat. Apparently I sat straight up and pointed to the doctor and said, "Look here, buddy, I am a preacher and I am a singer. DO NOT harm my throat; I have work to do."

I should have known then that God had a plan.

Unlike the first surgery, my recovery from this one seemed to be on fast forward. I was forming words again after days instead of weeks and months. Within a week I found myself trying to sing again.

Shortly after that was Christmas. I found myself in the back pew of a church where I didn't know anyone. The music to "O Holy Night" began to play. Remember my first solo at age three? It was to that song. This had to be a sign. I closed my eyes and at the same time opened my heart.

I asked God to allow my spirit to sing even if my mouth couldn't. Then the words spilled out. When the song was over, I opened my eyes and discovered that people were staring at me. So much for hiding.

I apologized profusely for singing too loudly. But the people were crying. They said they had never heard singing like that – that it was like angels were backing me up. I explained that they were and then gave my testimony.

The lady in front of me was dealing with cancer and had asked God for a sign. She got it through me.

When I returned to my surgeon for a follow-up, he and his intern began asking my husband questions. Finally I smiled and began answering them. The intern looked quickly at his chart, thinking he had the wrong one. He then asked, "Didn't you just have some of your tongue removed?"

I smiled and said yes. Then he looked at the doctor and said, "Should she be able to speak?"

The doctor replied "No," and smiled.

I looked at the intern and said, "What is medically impossible, is Heavenly possible."

–Pastor Wanda Christy-Shaner–

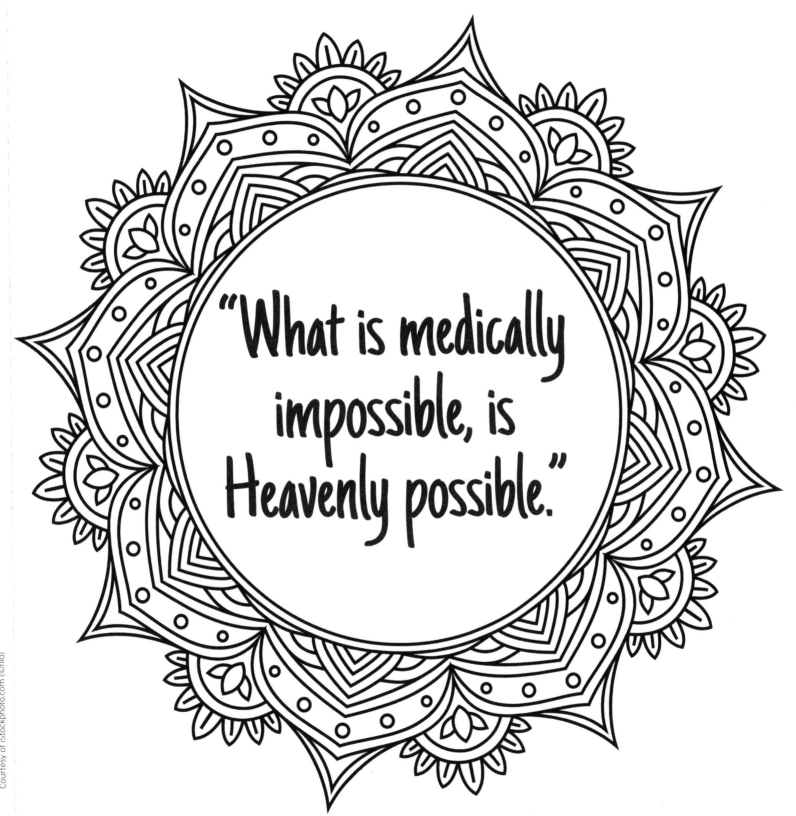

The Splendor of Spring

Where flowers bloom so does hope.
~Lady Bird Johnson

Is there anything more symbolic of spring, more emblematic of new life and renewal, than fruit trees bursting into blossom after a long Midwest winter? Sometimes, the only thought that sustains me through those dreaded months of shorter days and frigid temperatures is the certainty that the glory of spring will eventually return.

That's why, every fall, after the leaves have shriveled and the brilliant green of the garden has yielded to a dull, lifeless brown, I faithfully plant spring bulbs. Hope springs eternal, even in the Midwest. Thoughts of pastel blooms nodding in the gentle breeze enable me to overlook my chilled fingers and the lengthening shadows as I bury each bulb, wrapped in a winter "overcoat" of bone meal and rich soil. This climate definitely challenges my capacity for delayed gratification.

One fall, in addition to planting bulbs, my husband and I decided to add a pair of apricot trees to our yard. I could almost smell the sweetness of the blossoms and see the flower-laden branches reaching toward the sun. We weren't really concerned with harvesting a bountiful crop of apricots; it was the beauty of the blossoms that we anticipated.

That spring, while the apricot trees developed tiny, healthy-looking leaves, there were no blossoms, no heavenly aroma, no shower of petals as a brisk breeze suddenly stirred. We knew that it might take a few years for the blossoming to start. The rest of the garden was glorious, though, so we didn't mind waiting for nature to take its course with the apricot trees.

The second spring was a repeat of the previous one: still no flowering. The following year, the same thing. After nearly a dozen years, the trees became something of a joke: our "mock" apricot trees. In spite of fertilizing and pruning and treating them with the appropriate organic nutrients year after year, it seemed as though they had no intention of ever flowering.

And then one spring, in spite of the garden's pastel blues and pinks and purples, my world went dark. My husband died unexpectedly, shattering my world and everything in it. The brilliance of nature and the glory of spring seemed to mock me in my black cloud of grief.

Slowly, I realized that the blossoming, growing flowers and trees surrounding me might provide some consolation. I would try to appreciate the springtime that my husband and I had always treasured, as a tribute to him and the long hours he had invested in beautifying our surroundings.

A few mornings later, I took my coffee outside and watched the butterflies flit from tulip to tulip. Then I glanced to my right. Overnight, the apricot trees had burst into a riot of frothy blossoms. My heart skipped a beat. Clutching my coffee mug, I sat down on the garden bench before my knees buckled.

As the spring and summer progressed, tiny green buds of fruit began to form. The nurturing warmth of the sun developed them into ripened gold. When I picked each blushing apricot, I felt as though I was harvesting a tiny miracle. Day after day, I collected the fruit, and, before long, I had a refrigerator full of jam and a freezer loaded with preserves. For months to come, I savored the taste of summer each time I opened a jar.

The apricot trees never bloomed again. Somehow, I wasn't surprised. The blossoms were there when I needed them the most, to remind me of the promise of spring, of rebirth and eternal hope – and everlasting love.

–Joyce Styron Madsen–

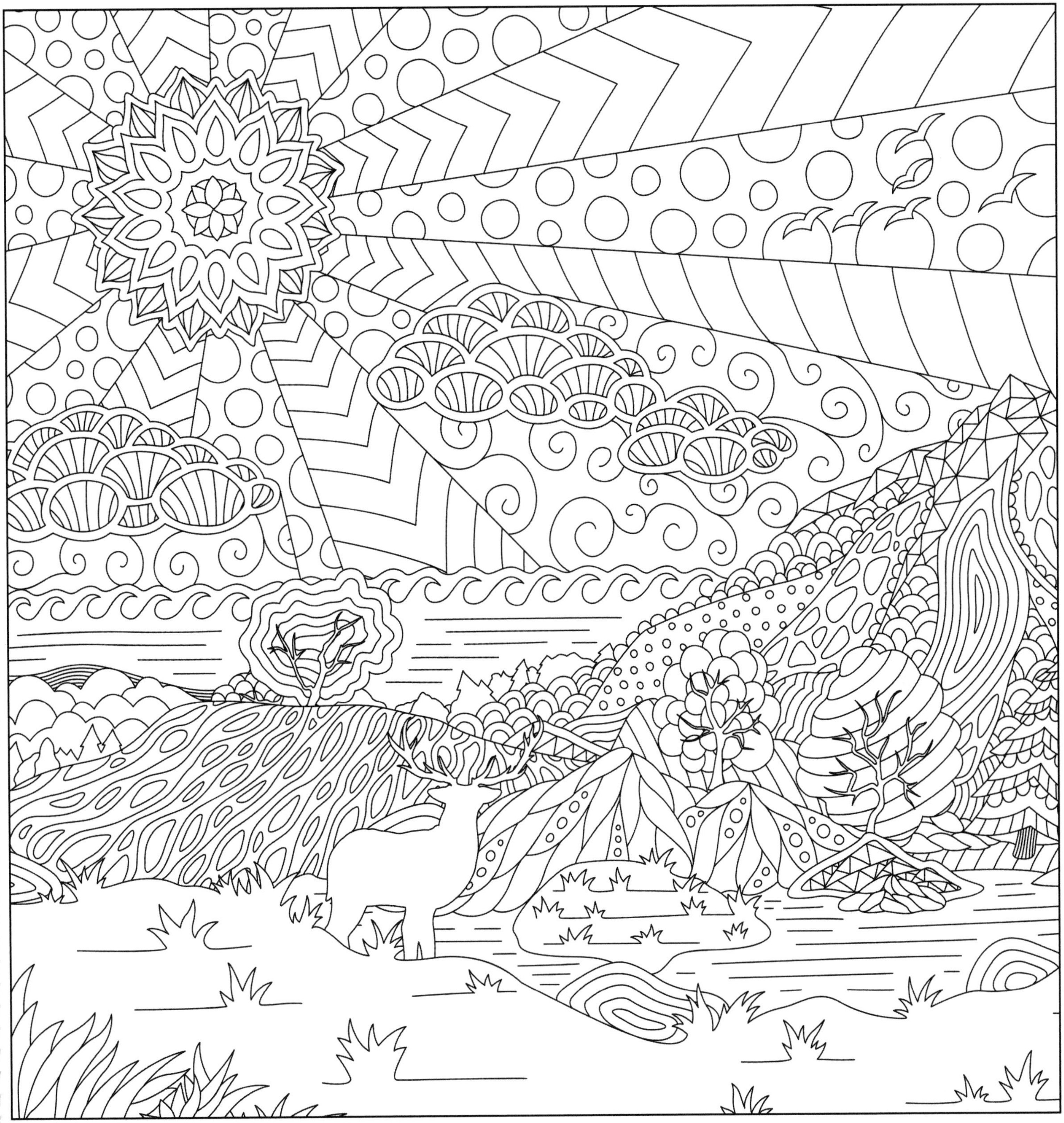

My Interstate Navigator

*Not everything we experience can be
explained by logic or science.
~Linda Westphal*

I was zooming down Interstate 80, heading east in Pennsylvania. The beautiful mountains covered with lush greenery loomed above both sides of the highway. Every few miles a farm appeared nestled among the rolling hills. It was a beautiful day with no weather issues and very little traffic.

But I couldn't really enjoy it. I was rushing to Lehigh Valley Hospital, where my mom had suffered a setback. She had called me at work just two hours before, crying that she needed me. As her daughter and a nurse, I couldn't ignore her plea. I left work and drove home to throw some clothes into a suitcase and let my husband know where I was going and why.

In an effort to calm my mother, I had promised her, "I'll be right there." What was I thinking? It was a three-hour trip.

Ahead I saw a large tractor-trailer laden with lumber. The load was held in place with multiple straps. As I looked at the trailer, I started to feel uneasy.

A voice said clearly, "Those straps are going to break."

"What?" I asked incredulously.

The voice elaborated. "The straps are going to break and that lumber is going to spill onto the road."

"Holy Mother of God!" I thought, panicked at what the voice was telling me. I was a few car lengths behind the truck and we were both moving at about seventy miles per hour.

The voice urged, "Pass him. Get away from him. Do it now!"

I obeyed, but when I pulled into the passing lane, the truck accelerated. This was creepy. I increased my speed enough to overtake the truck and kept an eye on the hazardous load.

Horrified, I watched as the straps holding the stacks of lumber in place started snapping, one by one, and twirling around uselessly in the air. Everything seemed to be happening in slow motion. When the third strap broke, the lumber started to shift.

The voice said authoritatively, "Pedal to the metal; get away from him as fast as you can."

I didn't question the voice. I floored it.

As my small sedan pulled away from that big truck, I watched the scene unfold in my rearview and side view mirrors. The stacks of wood rotated sideways and cascaded onto the road. The first pieces missed the back of my car by a few feet. I saw the truck slow down and could see the look of horror on the driver's face as he realized what was happening. He could clearly see the lumber slide off his truck onto both eastbound lanes of Route 80.

I safely pulled away and my speed returned to normal as I viewed the spectacle in the rearview mirror. I watched as the trucker brought his vehicle to a stop.

I offered up a prayer of thanks for having heard the voice. There was no doubt in my mind that God was my navigator on the interstate that day.

— Nancy Emmick Panko—

The feeling this dog gave me — that everything was going to be all right — was not a guarantee that Betsy would not die of cancer nor that we weren't going to suffer; rather it seemed the assurance that, whatever happened, we were not going through it alone.

Excerpt from "The White Dog" by Joshua J. Mark, a story in *Chicken Soup for the Soul: Angels & Miracles*

The Blessing of Fear

Is it possible that a miracle could lie hidden, dormant for years, like a frightened wildflower seed – waiting and waiting for the right time to grow and make itself known? Its path, blown by the winds, burying it beneath the soil until the day that God says, "It's time." Finally, it sprouts and pushes through, reaching, no longer encumbered by its earthly bounds, only to bless the world with its colors and scent.

Fears are like seeds, too, mere shells or wrappings to break out of if you view them with the right perspective, waiting to transform into miracles if you really look at them.

It was a long time coming for me, but that's what I did. I faced a fear and visited the Metropolitan State Mental Hospital in Norwalk, California, the place where my mom had been a patient back in the mid 1970's. I was fourteen at the time and visited her there only once, but I remember it well. As though it were yesterday.

Soon after ending her stay there.... she ended her own life. I never got to say goodbye. Years later the aforementioned became "the seed" for my art, my writing, my passion for helping others. But, much like the wildflower seed, I needed to push past my earthly boundaries. Hence, my visit there that day.

During my visit I was drawn to a particular set of dilapidated old buildings, which were built over 100 years ago. Some say they are haunted, and from the looks of them I would be inclined to agree. On the other side of the mile-square property are several other buildings, still used today. These house the criminally insane, among others. Many sheriff deputies were on high alert and, of course, wondering why I was there when I appeared one day. But I explained my mission and with raised eyebrows they sent me on my way.

Soon I discovered the abandoned building my mom once resided in. It seemed to be calling me as it sat stoic, even in disrepair, covered in vines. Its broken windows peered back with a blank stare that I am sure many of its long ago patients also shared. In spite of my reluctance I entered the building. The eerie ambiance was straight out of the movies. Long pitch-black hallways, old brick arches and well-worn linoleum floors spread throughout. The giant catacomb of rooms was dark, dreary, dusty and trashed. A wild cat or two scurried about, as did my heart.

Soon I found the very same room that my mother once called home for a while, with the same teal colored paint I remembered so well, now cracked and peeling. Brighter unblemished patches of paint shone where pictures once hung like windows to the past. Oh what these walls must have seen.

And then it hit me – many things I had put to rest came flooding back in an avalanche of emotion. Cascading memories flickered by so fast that it made it hard to focus. Were these windows to the past really working?

I reflected for a moment, letting everything sink in. I thought of forgiveness. I thought of the good and the bad, the memories. And, I thought of my mom's fondness for horses – a result perhaps of her having grown up very close to Santa Anita racetrack.

I looked into the shadows and saw something. A small plastic horse lying in a corner covered in dust, a symbolic reminder of why I was there. A gift, if you will, for facing my fears. I can't put into words all the emotions I was feeling, other than to say that my visit there felt like an atomic bomb of emotional confetti going off. A bomb of closure, healing, sadness, and yes, strangely enough... joy... all at once. I finally got to say goodbye.

One of the hardest things I have ever done was to visit there that day. Yet I needed to do it. And thus, I received the miracle of closure – in a brief instant... an instant that took forty years.

When you face your fears, they become your strength to receive the miracles laid out before you. And this is when God says, "It's time."

– Stan Holden –

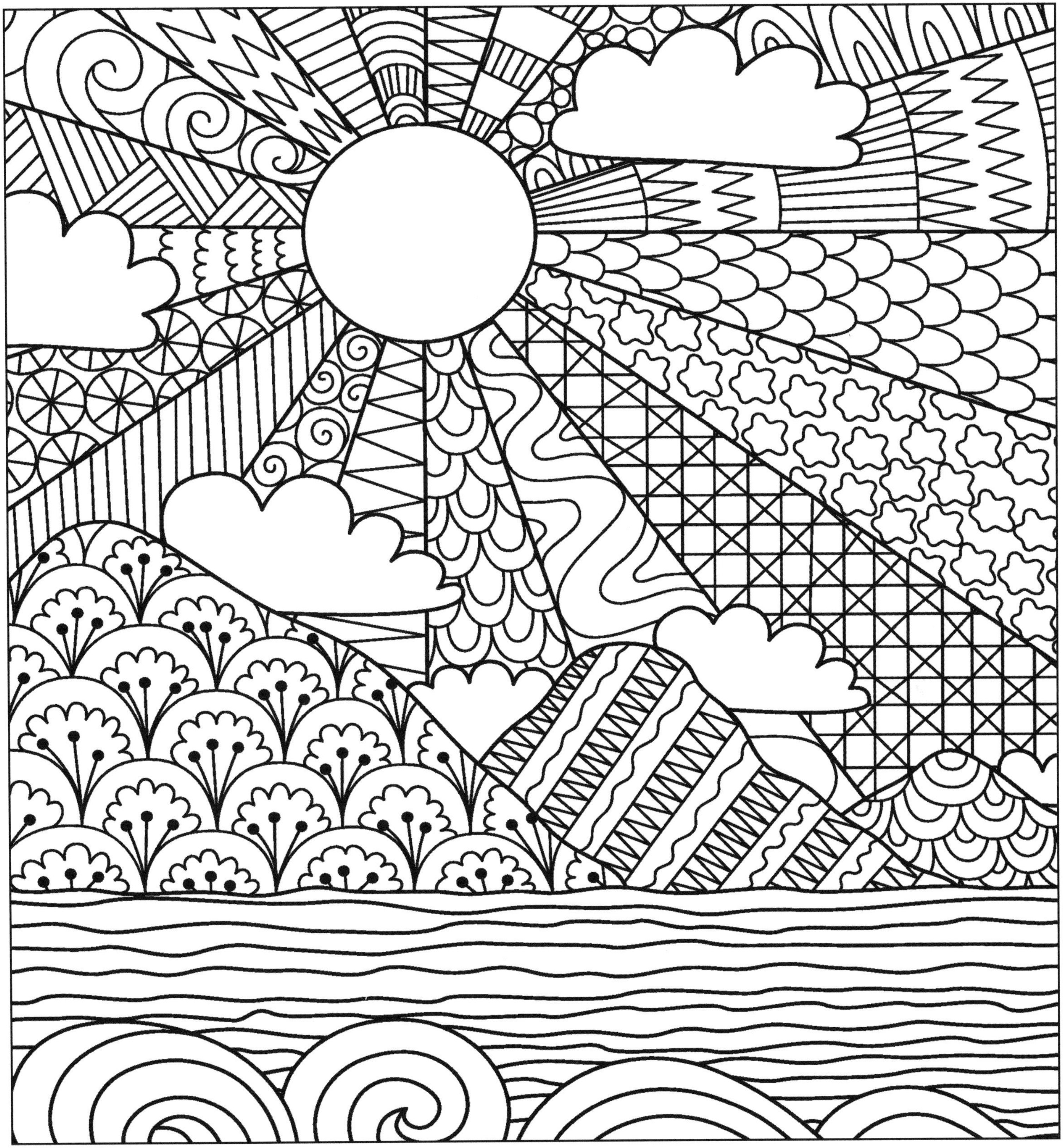

Spidey Senses

Brothers are like streetlights along the road; they don't make distance any shorter but they light up the path and make the walk worthwhile.
~Author Unknown

It was the morning of our seventh wedding anniversary, and my husband and I were ecstatic. I had just taken a pregnancy test, and the results were positive!

A few months earlier, my fertility specialist had gravely stated that, after a year of failed treatment, I "should not expect to be a biological mother."

We decided not to tell anyone until we were sure there was no chance of losing the baby. My first pregnancy had ended in an unexpected miscarriage that required emergency surgery, leaving us devastated. As happy as we were, we decided to exercise caution.

Just then, the phone rang. It was my youngest brother, Wade. Wade and I were very close and spoke regularly. Our two older brothers affectionately referred to us as "The Witch Mountain Twins," likening us to the stars of the Disney film because of the way our thoughts seemed connected. Wade and I had always joked that we had "spidey senses." Knowing this, my husband immediately said, "Don't tell... not even Wade."

I answered the phone as normally as I could. It was Sunday, and Wade was confirming plans we had to meet up the following Saturday. After a few minutes of casual conversation, Wade became serious and said, "Can I ask you something kind of personal?' I laughed and replied sure.

Wade lowered his voice and asked, "Are you pregnant?"

I paused and answered truthfully, "According to Dr. Gill, no... maybe not ever. Why?"

Wade continued, "This is going to sound crazy. I have had this feeling all morning. It's almost like I'm remembering a dream, only I didn't dream it. I'm sitting here, drinking coffee, and it's like I just know it."

"Know what?" I asked.

"That our spidey senses are changing. You know... that thing we do. Don't get me wrong. It's not that we won't be close anymore, but more like some of that ability is being transferred to a child. Your child. I feel like you're going to have a baby soon. This sounds crazy, but I just know you are. Are you sure you're not pregnant?"

I was astonished. The moment I learned I was pregnant, Wade knew.

I had promised my husband I wouldn't tell. So I replied, "Wade, I'd love for that to be true. But I've just spent hundreds of dollars for the top fertility specialist in Houston to tell me – in his words – that I shouldn't expect to have kids. Let's just leave it at that."

Wade replied in a voice of absolute certainty, "Well, they're wrong."

Four months later, we announced we were pregnant with a baby girl. Before I told Wade, I asked him if he remembered our conversation from that day in October. He did. So it was no surprise when I told him I was pregnant that he simply replied, "I knew. But I was going to let you tell me when you were ready."

I gave birth to a beautiful baby girl five months later. And now that five years have passed, I often think about the words my brother spoke to me that day, about our "ability" transferring to a child. Wade and I still have a special bond, but like he said, it is different now. And some days, when my daughter looks at me with her beautiful, soulful blue eyes, I wonder if his prediction has already come true.

– Jolie Lisenby–

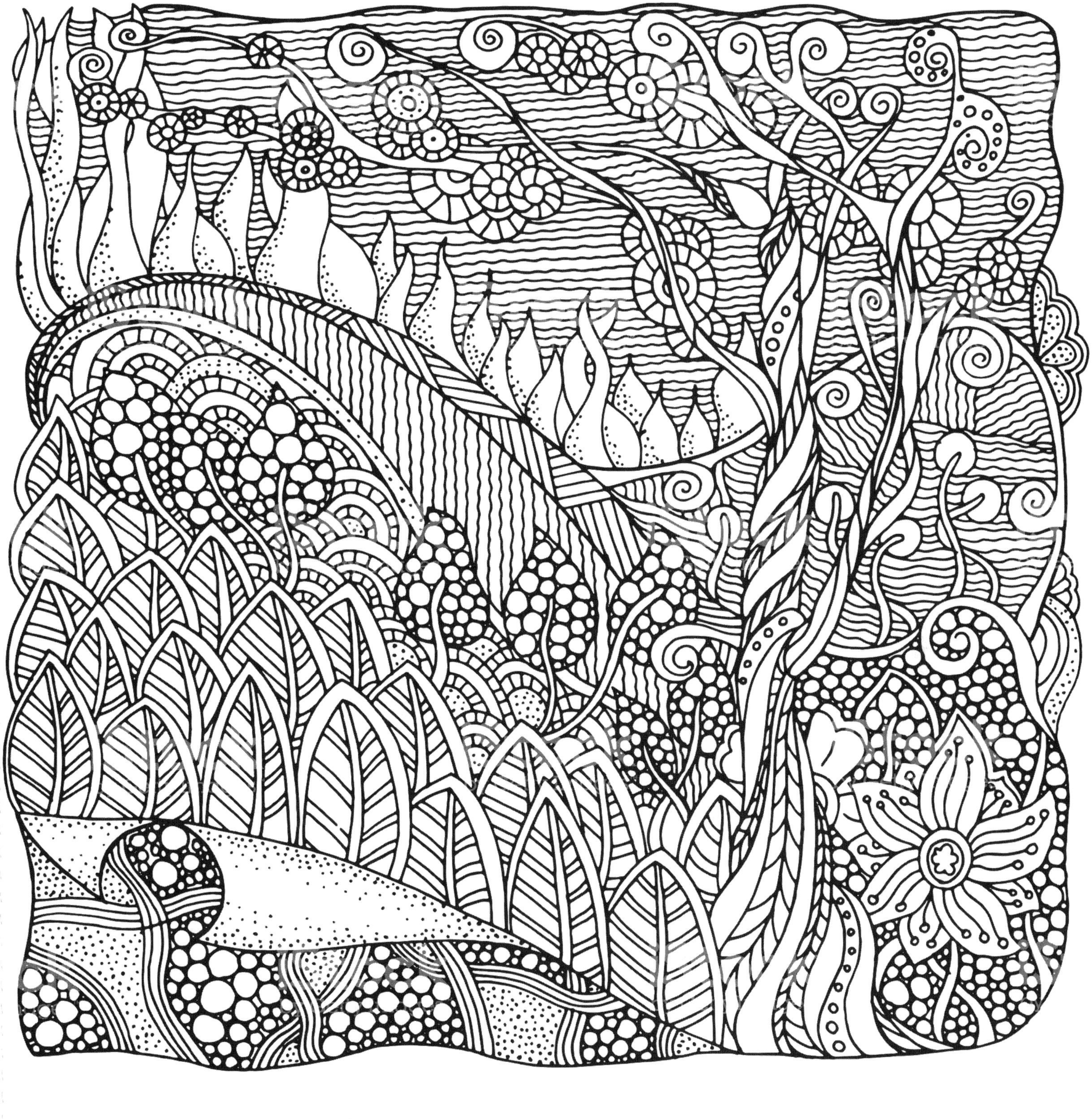

Courtesy of iStockphoto.com (©elfiny)

Just a Dream Away

My grandmother is my angel on earth.
~Catherine Pulsifer

I was sitting on a wood bench in a garden filled with daisies, which were my grandmother's favorite flower. The sun was shining and felt warm on my skin. The air had a faint smell of sandalwood and vanilla. It was the unmistakable aroma of my grandmother's favorite perfume. She had passed away several years before, and I still missed her terribly.

All of a sudden I could hear her voice. It started off faint, like a whisper, and continued to grow louder and louder. "Wake up, you need to put him in his crib." She just kept saying it over and over, getting more and more frantic. Was she here? Her presence seemed so real.

The sunny sky turned dark and lightning began to shoot all around me. All of a sudden, I felt two frail hands grab my shoulders and shake me violently. I heard my grandmother's voice again: "Please wake up; you need to put him in his crib. There is not much time."

I woke up in a cold sweat. There were tears streaming down my face. It took me a moment to collect myself and figure out where I was. The room was dark, except for the glow of the television. I could hear the rain hitting the roof. I had fallen asleep watching cartoons on the couch again. I looked over at the recliner and saw my one-year-old sleeping peacefully, curled up under his favorite blanket. The thunder boomed outside and I decided that the sounds of the storm must have been responsible for my nightmare. I crawled off of the couch and went to get a glass of water.

As I entered the kitchen the lights started to flicker. I heard another loud burst of thunder and my electricity turned off completely. All of a sudden, my grandmother's words echoed through my mind. "You need to put him in his crib. There is not much time."

I walked back into the living room and went over to the recliner. I scooped my little man up into my arms. He nuzzled his head into my chest as I cradled him closer. I walked slowly to his room, navigating through the dark hallway, trying hard not to wake him. He smelled like lavender baby lotion. His eyelids fluttered and he smiled as he slept. I laid him in the crib, covered him with a blanket, and kissed him on his forehead. I whispered, "I love you more than pigs love slop." This was an old saying my grandfather had always told us. I stood there in the dark staring at him. I brushed my hand across his forehead and kissed him one more time.

As I was leaving his room, the entire house shook. There was a loud crash followed by the sound of wind and rushing water. My heart started pounding so fast I thought it was going to jump right out of my chest. I quickly looked back over to the crib. My son was still sleeping peacefully. I ran into the hallway. The wind was ripping through the house. I could feel the temperature dropping. When I reached the living room I saw a sight that brought me to my knees. A giant tree limb was sticking into the house through the bay window. It had landed right on the recliner that my son had been sleeping on moments before. There was broken glass everywhere. The wind and rain poured through the broken window. I ran over and tried to move the tree limb. I tried to push it back outside, but it was thick and heavy. I began shaking and crying hysterically. The reality of the situation hit me like a ton of bricks. If my son had still been lying on that recliner, his little body would have been crushed under the immense weight of the tree limb.

When the storm ended and the sun came back out, we inspected the tree. A bolt of lightning had hit it and severed the limb, which sent it flying through my bay window. The force and impact were enough to do severe damage to the house and ruin several pieces of furniture. All of that could be repaired or replaced. I felt immensely grateful that my son was sleeping soundly in his crib when the branch came crashing in. I believe that my grandmother came to me in my dream that night, to save her great-grandson's life.

−Tiffany O'Connor−

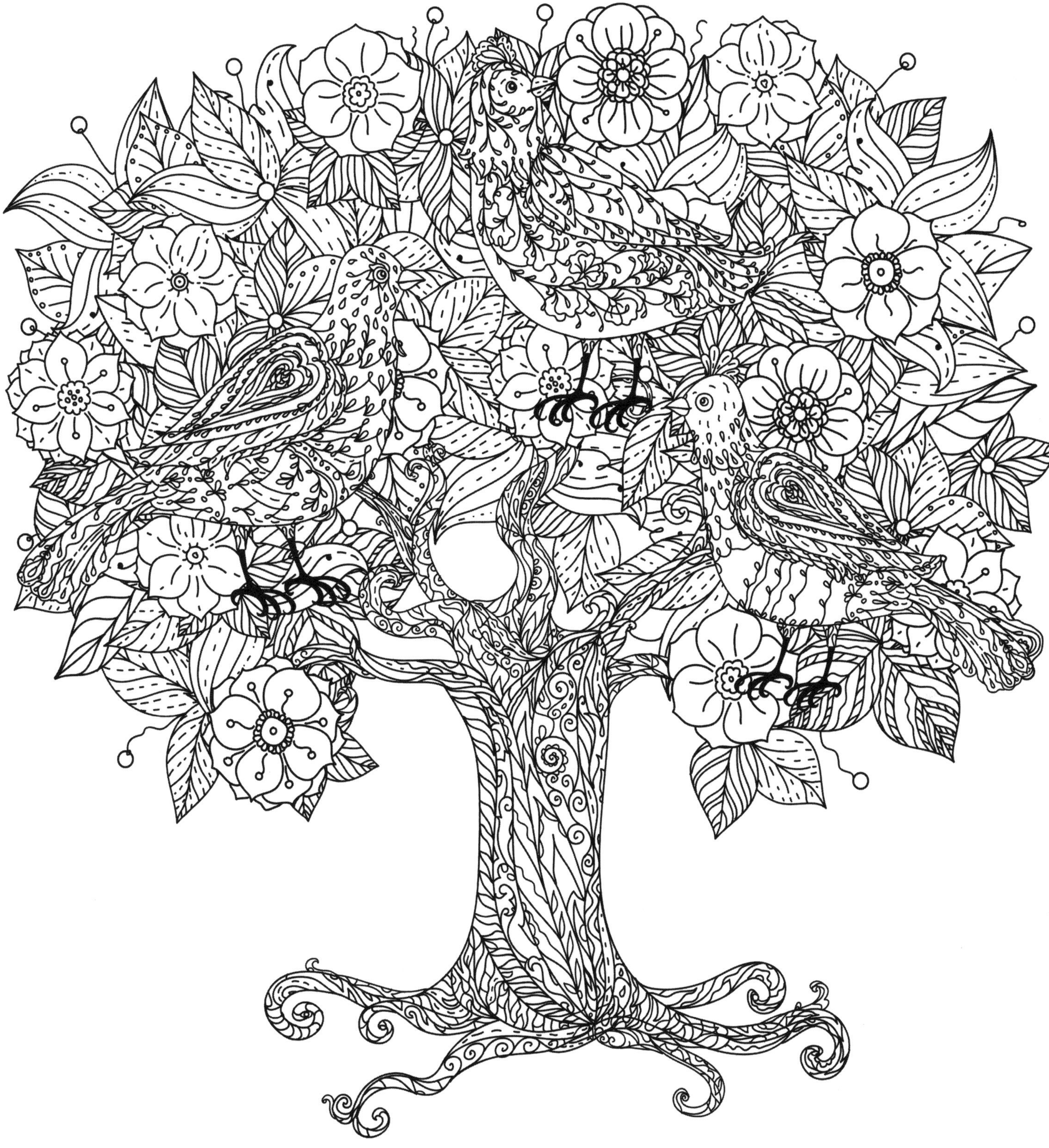

When I told John of the diagnosis, he didn't hesitate. That's when my sixty-year-long miracle began. And that's when I first heard John utter those magic words: "Of course we're still getting married! We'll live as though you don't have it and go ahead with our lives expecting the best. If we expect the worst, we'll probably get it. But if we hope for the best we're more likely to get that. Attitude is a very powerful medicine."

Excerpt from "A Husband's Magic Words" by Toni Somers, a story in *Chicken Soup for the Soul: Angels & Miracles*

Fun Up Here

Perhaps they are not stars, but rather openings in heaven
where the love of our lost ones pours
through and shines down upon us to
let us know they are happy.
~Inuit Proverb

I dressed my ever growing body in stretchy dress clothes and headed out for another day at the office. As I began my thirty-minute commute, I quickly drove by my parents' house two streets over and noticed my mother's black sedan parked in the driveway. I recalled she had mentioned the prior evening that she was experiencing a headache. I cracked a smile and called her to poke fun at her for playing hooky from work for a mere headache. The phone wasn't answered.

I had a new employee starting, and things were busy at work. But a couple of hours later I phoned again. There was still no answer. For reasons I will never be able to explain, I got a sinking feeling in my stomach. I called my father, and although he thought I was being overly dramatic, he drove home to check on my mother.

She was gone, at age sixty-three. A massive aneurysm had killed her.

I remember yelling, "How could this happen? I'm nine months pregnant!" I had experienced two miscarriages, and this miracle baby was days away from arriving – my mother's first grandchild.

The night after my mother passed, my best friend had a dream and she desperately wanted to tell me about it. I was not emotionally stable enough, so I politely asked her if she could share her dream with me another time.

Twelve days later, my son was born. It was surreal. I had lost my mother, and now I was a mother. I didn't know how I could possibly collect myself enough to take care of another human being. I wanted my mom. I wanted her to meet her grandson. I felt alone, and I felt intensely angry that she was gone.

Weeks went by and I tried to settle into a routine, but in all honesty, it was a very trying time.

Again my friend nagged me to let her tell me about her dream. I finally relented and said, "I will try to listen."

"In my dream your mom appeared holding the hands of two children. The boy was taller and older than the girl. Your mom said, 'Tell Nicole we are having fun up here.'"

I wept. My mother was in heaven taking care of the two children I had miscarried. I was wrong the entire time – she might not have met my third child yet, but she got to meet the first two children, the ones I hadn't known. There was a sense of relief that my children were in the hands of the best mother I have ever known.

I still grieve, and I still have incredibly difficult days, but I smile thinking about my three loves up in heaven. My angels are "having fun up here."

–Nicole Vickers–

The Polar Bears

Diane was the youngest of the four of us. She was a bit of a rebel, but you couldn't help but love her. She was funny, strong, smart, talented, beautiful, and passionate.

One of her passions was protecting polar bears! She was in awe that such strong, dominant animals were seen as symbols of acceptance in some cultures. Fascinated with spiritual stories, she believed as they did, that in order to survive, the polar bear allowed spirits to whiten his coat to blend with the snow. "His acceptance," she confirmed, "is a sign of his strength." Diane would tuck photos of polar bears inside random cards that she would send when she knew someone needed words of support.

No one ever thought Diane would die of an accidental overdose, much less get hooked on drugs. A crippling accident in her twenties had introduced her to pain medications and she couldn't overcome her addiction.

My brother and I had said goodbye to our parents, our older brother, and many relatives and friends, but Diane's passing released too many emotions too quickly. For years we danced around our emotions. Holidays were the most difficult.

One particular Thanksgiving would be no different. It had been a long day visiting my younger brother and his family. Somehow, we couldn't stop talking about Diane, arguing about her, trying to resolve so many unanswered questions. We were angry with her and we hadn't been able to forgive her for the way she died.

I started my long drive home from my brother's house still haunted by thoughts of my sister's passing. "It will be a long night adding to the long day," I thought.

Halfway home, I realized I had forgotten to buy a birthday card for a dear friend who never forgot mine. I only knew of one grocery store close to home that would be open and fortunately, they sold cards. So, as midnight approached, I took the exit that detoured me to the "24/7" store.

The store was practically empty, just a few shoppers filling their baskets. I had the card aisle all to myself until I felt the presence of someone next to me. She was an old woman, dressed in a turquoise and gold sari. Her face was veiled, exposing only her dark, penetrating, yet gentle eyes. The deep, weathered wrinkles that encircled them revealed she was an old soul. "Here," she said in a soft Indian accent, "I believe these cards are for you!" She handed me two cards.

I thanked her, and looked down at the cards, which were the same. On the front was a photo of a polar bear with his giant paw across his eyes. When you opened the card there were only two visible words, "I'm sorry!"

I immediately knew what this was. It was a message from Diane – her way of letting us know she was sorry and that it was time for both of us to heal and to forgive. I turned to thank the old woman again, but she was gone. I raced through the store, up and down aisles asking the few shoppers and employees if anyone had seen her. No one remembered the old woman in the turquoise and gold sari.

I knew this was no coincidence. Diane was saying she was sorry. But there was more to it. Staring at the photos of the polar bears, I remembered her symbolic story of how they accepted a white coat of fur in order to survive in their snow-covered domain. I heard my sister's voice reminding me, "There is strength in acceptance!" I knew then, her real message for my brother and me, was about acceptance. It was the key component that was missing for our survival as well. In order to forgive and heal, we needed to accept not only Diane's way of life but also her death.

The next day, I mailed my brother his card with a lengthy note explaining how I received it. He understood and accepted the miracle that I had witnessed. Years have passed and we have healed, but my polar bear card from heaven remains on my fireplace mantle enclosed with my own personal note to my little sister: Apology accepted!

–Lainie Belcastro–

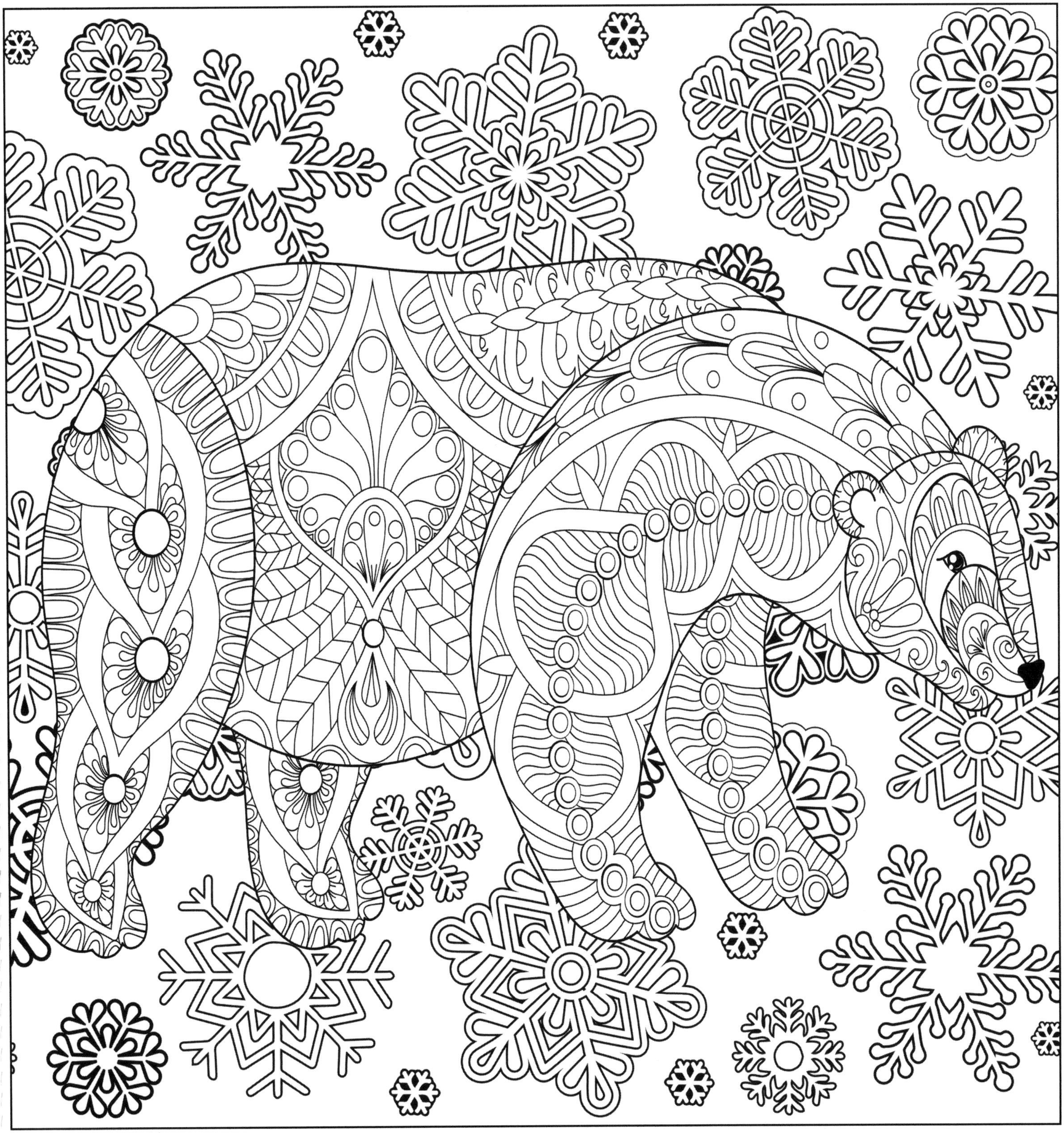

The Last Message

My memory of that night comes in bright white flashes. I remember the back door opening. I remember "Silent Night" by Mannheim Steamroller playing on the radio. I remember a glass snowman filled with chocolate kisses sitting on an end table in the den. I remember Daniel's face and his anger. I remember him telling me that Julie was gone.

I remember not understanding. "Where did she go? What do you mean she's gone?" I remember my son looking me in the eye and saying, "She's just gone." And then I remember him falling to the floor.

Daniel has juvenile diabetes, so you can imagine how I felt the night the back door slammed shut and he collapsed. I was sure it was the diabetes. I remember shouting at him and screaming for someone to help.

After that, we couldn't get Daniel out of bed. He wouldn't cry. He just lay there and slept. On the second day, the principal of his school called me and told me he expected Daniel in school that day. I thought the principal was being callous.

It wasn't until I pulled up in front of the school that I understood why the principal had called. There were hundreds of students waiting for Daniel to arrive. They needed him; he needed them. They surrounded him and vanished with him into the school. For the remaining days of the school year students were constantly monitoring my son. He was never alone. Never.

Days later, letters would arrive in mailboxes addressed by Julie to various people who were important to her. In those letters she apologized for what she had done. She expressed her deep sorrow and concern for those she left behind. She urged friends to keep succeeding and wished them happy and fulfilling lives. She didn't ask them to understand why she took her own life.

I was there when my son's letter arrived. I sat beside him as he read her words written in a yellow card decorated with daisies. He folded the card and slipped it back into its envelope. I've never seen it since.

Everywhere I looked there was sadness. My son was inconsolable. I looked to heaven and cried. I begged for answers and sobbed for relief for my son.

The funeral was approaching. It was creeping up on us like a cat stalking its prey. Where to go? What to do? The mall was safe. It was normal. It was "away."

People briskly walked by chatting and laughing. Teenage girls flipped their hair and giggled. Mothers pushed strollers with sleeping children while toddlers tugged at their fathers' hands. You could smell a mixture of popcorn and cinnamon in the air. No sadness, no gut-wrenching grief. Safe.

My son, my husband and I walked down the hallway of the mall as if we were weighed down by 500 pounds of pain. We watched normalcy unfold in front of us. It hurt. I thought I saw Julie in a group of girls walking away from me. No. I just wanted to know if she was all right.

We three sat together on a bench, staring at our shoes. We said nothing. We were so tired.

I looked up. There were two men standing in front of us... just normal guys dressed in plaid flannel shirts with their sleeves rolled up. They wore jeans and what we called "Chucks," high top sneakers. The tall one stood back while the shorter dark haired one leaned forward and grabbed my hand. I recoiled, but he firmly grasped my fingers and said, "She's okay. We've been sent to tell you she's okay. She is with God and everything is fine."

I turned to look at my husband's startled face. I looked back. They were gone... disappeared into thin air.

I saw them. My husband saw them. But most of all, my son saw them. And we all heard him.

I always thought of angels as winged spirits with halos who flutter to earth in a shining glow of light and love. Not so. These were ordinary, approachable men who blended in with everyone else. There was no heralding trumpet, no glow of a halo – just ordinary guys sent to deliver a loving, reassuring last message.

–Rebecca Newman–

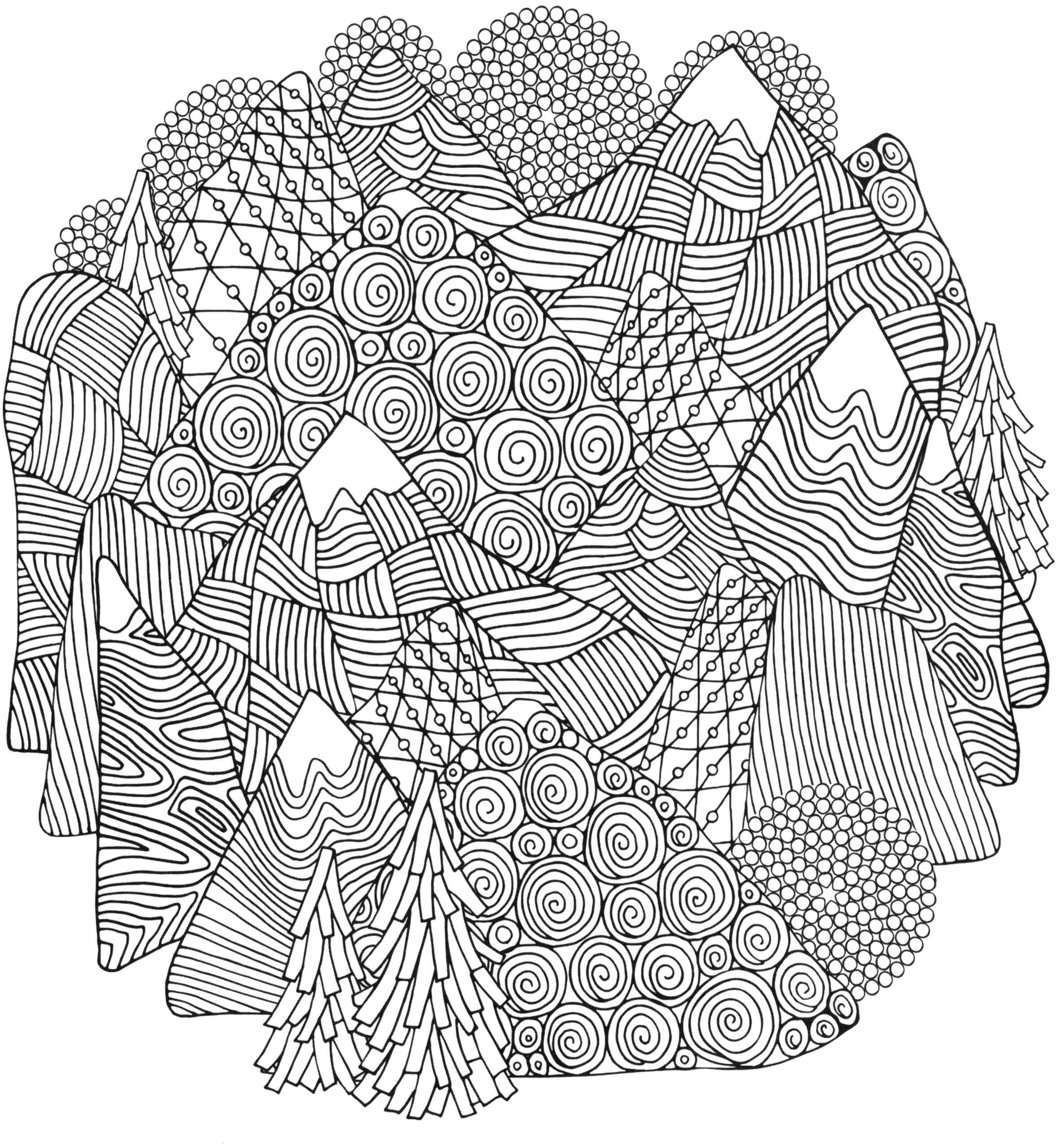

Midnight Prayer

*Silently, one by one, in the infinite meadows
of the heaven, blossomed the lovely stars,
the forget-me-nots of the Angels.
~Henry Wadsworth Longfellow*

Last night I looked up at the sky
I wished that you were near
It's been a while since I have prayed
But God, I need an ear.

I'm worried that my angel
Is too far for me to see
What if one day Heaven
Hasn't saved a spot for me?

And suddenly I heard a voice
God whispered "There's no hurry."
He said, "Your angel waits for you,
You'll never have to worry.

The stars above are porch lights
That welcome old friends home
So when it's time for you to come
You'll never feel alone.

I promise that he waits for you
So never shed a tear,
Your angel keeps his porch light on
Until the day you're here.

To remind you that he's waiting
He lights up like a beam,
And when you are so deep in sleep
He slips into your dream.

He watches you each morning,
Protects when you feel scared,
He guides you through each journey,
Gives strength when unprepared.

The sunrays are his warm hugs,
The rain is his soft cry,
For times that you doubt Heaven,
Or wish he'd said goodbye.

But angels never leave us,
Although they're not in sight,
They wake us up each morning,
and tuck us in each night.

So though he may seem far away,
When it's your time just know,
Your angel will be upon his porch,
Singing "Welcome Home."

–Samantha Nolan–

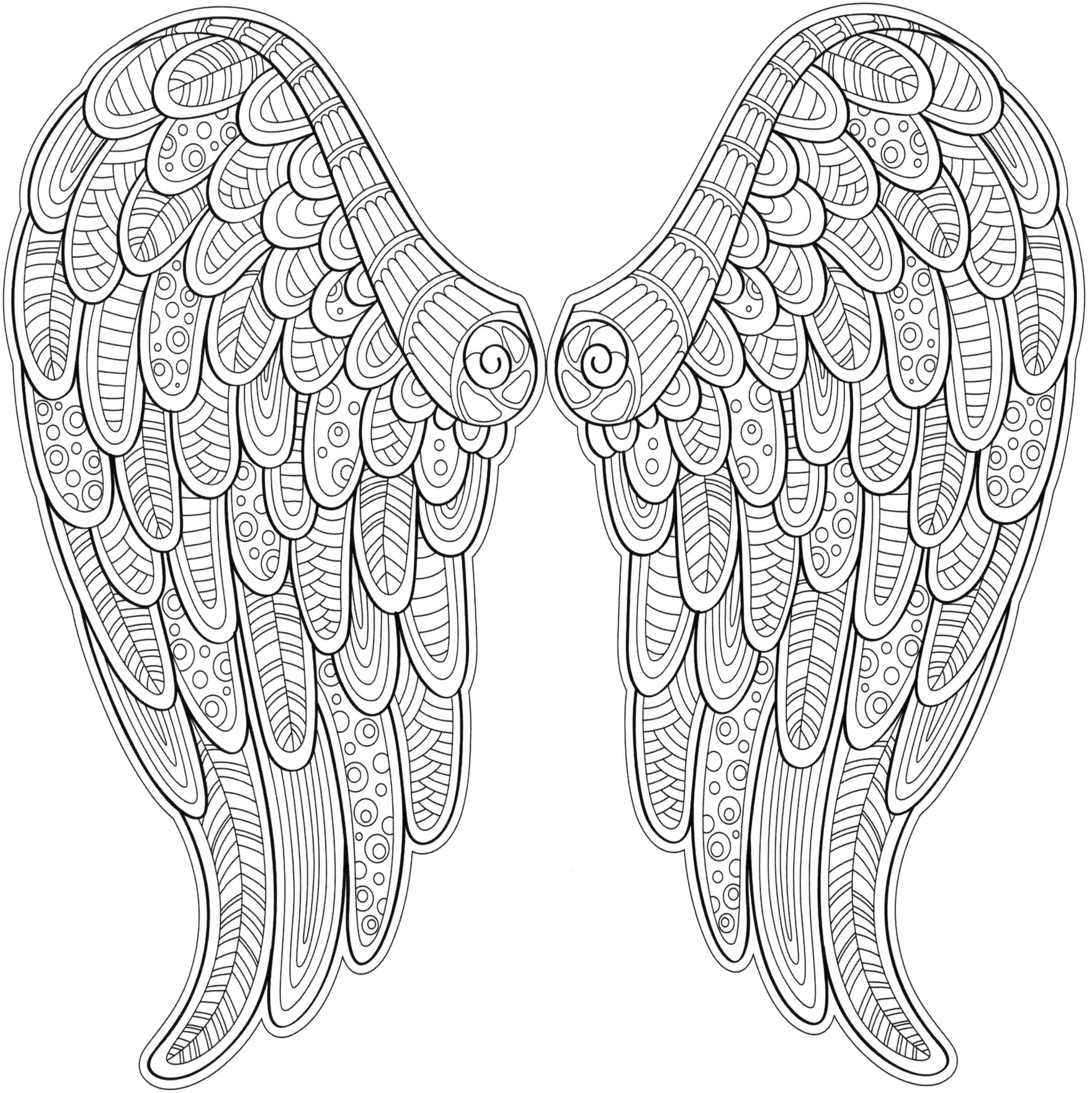

Everything brought memories of my sweet husband and the life that we had lived together. But I was no longer afraid of the memories. I knew that he still wanted me to see all the beauty of the world, just as he had when he was here with me. I could feel his presence in the woods now as a peaceful, guiding spirit, pointing out all the beautiful sights and sounds just as he did in life.

Excerpt from "Wonders of Nature" by Betsy S. Franz, a story in *Chicken Soup for the Soul: Angels & Miracles*

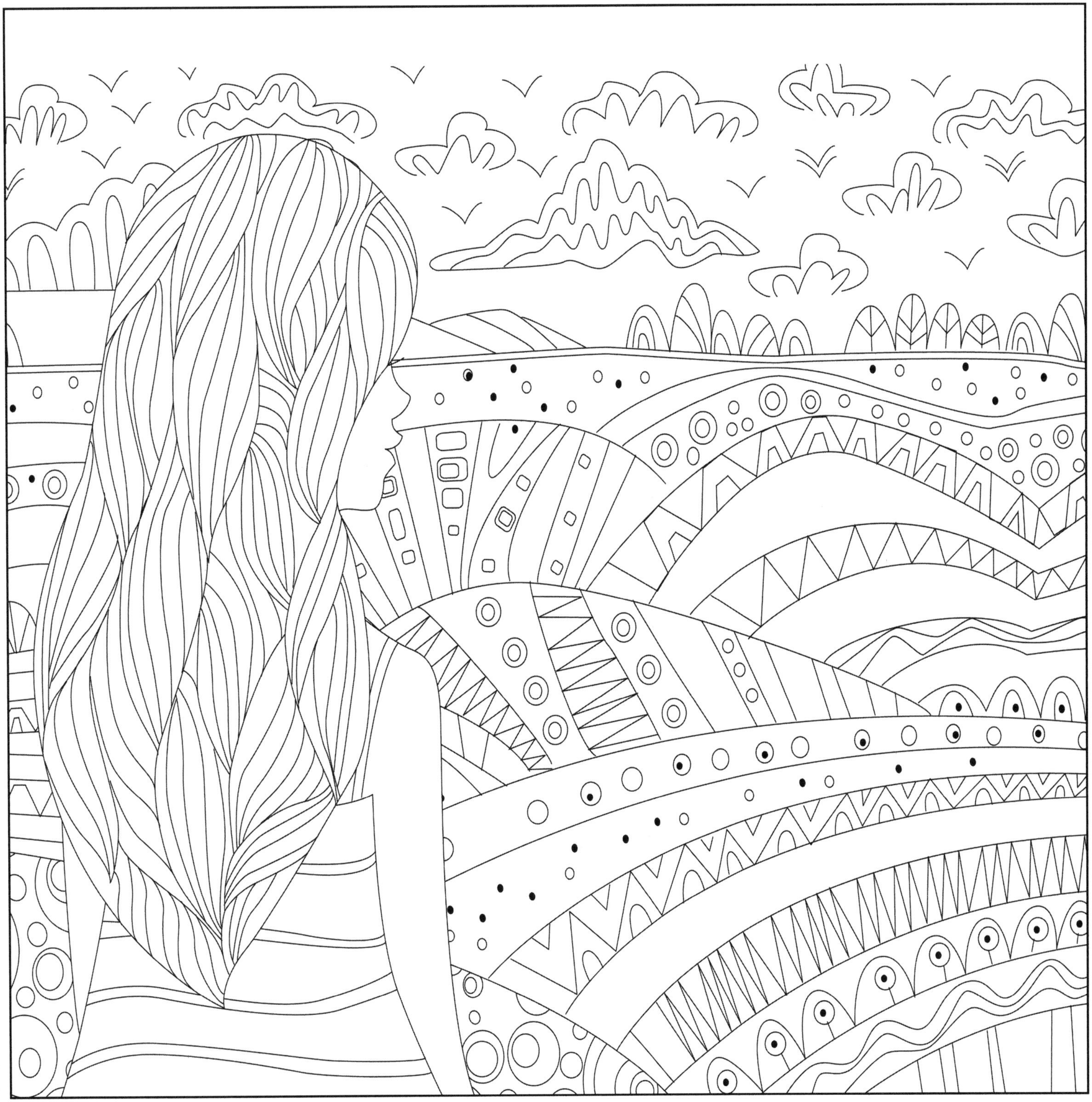

A New Trust

*Ask the LORD your God for a sign, whether in the deepest
depths or in the highest heights.*
~Isaiah 7:11

I had just graduated from college and I went from May to July without even a single callback from prospective employers. It seemed that my skills as an English major might be useless. I was starting to doubt everything I studied and the path I pursued. "Maybe I should've chosen a safer path," I thought. My parents, who were paying my bills at the time, were starting to get anxious about my unemployment and things were getting tense between us.

One night, after spending time with friends, I pulled into my parents' driveway and decided to take a walk instead of going inside. It was late and I knew they would be asleep. The neighborhood was quiet as I walked to my old elementary school, only a couple of minutes away. The gates were open, so I let my mind wander as I looked at the building, the playground, and the playing fields. I had worked so hard to get through school, all the way up to my bachelor's degree, and yet I felt as far away from my future as I did when I was ten years old. I needed help and didn't know where to get it.

I walked over to the baseball field where I used to play and looked up at the sky. I searched for the right words, but all I could think of were curses. It had been a very long time since I looked up for answers and I had practically forgotten how to do it. Finally, more out of desperation than anger, I said out loud, "God, if you have a plan for me, I'd like to see the blueprints." I then left the school grounds and headed back home.

I decided to take a different, longer path back to the house. As I walked, I noticed almost all the streetlights were out. There was one still lit, however, and as I passed under it I noticed something shiny on the ground. It was a penny. As I picked it up, I noticed another penny, and another, and another. Searching the street and the grass I found nearly a dollar's worth of pennies scattered under this one light. I was in shock. I had never seen so much change on the ground. Somehow, it filled me with hope. I suddenly felt like everything was going to be okay, even though a dollar was not going to solve any of my financial problems. "Maybe my luck will turn around," I thought. I pocketed all the change and returned home in a brighter mood.

A week later, I saw an ad in the newspaper for a job. The position called for a writer/proofreader for a local magazine called *The Pennysaver*. I thought back to that night on the street and felt like this could be the one. I sent in my résumé, got a call three days later, and got the job by the end of August. I couldn't believe it!

I was fortunate to stay with that job for seven years before moving on to my dream job of teaching. And ever since that night, I have regained trust in the universe and how things fall into place.

Whenever I'm in doubt and feel like nothing will go my way, I look for signs, not out of desperation or fear but out of trust. I trust that anything is possible as long as I believe it is and as long as I keep my eyes open.

That night I felt like I was being watched over. In a lot of ways, I still carry that same awe of seeing all those pennies on the ground, and to this day I chuckle to myself every time I pick one up.

—Mike D'Alto—

I have regained trust in the universe and how things fall into place.

White Feathers

As soon as I saw the small feather angel on the car floor, I knew it was a bad omen. It always hung from my mirror and even with the air conditioning on full blast, the angel had always stayed put.

My husband John had been in the hospital for almost three months, and even though the doctors stressed that his situation was severe, there had never been any doubt in my mind that he would make it home. Now I wasn't so sure.

This had been a month of deaths. My father's cousin had passed away unexpectedly and now my cousin Roy was dying of lung cancer. I was praying for him to make it, not only because he was my cousin, but because I am a highly superstitious person and I believe that things happen in threes. If my cousin died, I was sure John would be next. When I received the phone call that Roy had passed away I ran to the bathroom and threw up my breakfast.

Now I picked up the angel and tried to hang it on the mirror again, but it wouldn't stay put. It kept falling down, so I put it on the car seat. In a daze, I started the car and pulled out of the parking lot. I caught myself singing burial hymns on the way to the hospital. This really freaked me out and I almost hit the car in front of me as I stepped on the gas instead of the brakes. I was hoping it was not a sign, but deep down I was certain that John would not make it after all.

When I got to the hospital, I received bad news. My husband wasn't going to make it. Five days later he passed away and I fell to pieces.

After being cooped up in my apartment alone for an entire week, not wanting to talk to anyone, it felt like the walls were closing in on me. My son had gone back to his life and I realized that I needed to face the world again, too. I wasn't ready to return to work, but I needed to get out of my apartment before I lost my mind.

It was a beautiful summer day so I decided to take a long walk. I started on the walking trail behind the apartment building, my head down, afraid to run into someone I knew. I suddenly noticed white feathers scattered to my right. I didn't pay too much attention at first but every time I turned onto a new path, left or right, there were more white feathers, always scattered on my right. For the last fifteen years I had walked these paths almost daily and had never seen any white feathers, and now they were everywhere.

My spirits lifted immediately. I knew at that moment that somebody was looking out for me, and I hoped it was John. During the following weeks I saw feathers every time I went for a walk, even when I chose a different route. However, as the weeks passed they were more scattered. By now I was certain they were a sign from above.

After two weeks my boss called and encouraged me to come back to work. "You don't need to do anything," he said. "But I think you need to be around other people."

He was right, of course. Living on a military base in another country, I didn't have any family members close by. And talking to them on the phone wasn't the same as being with them. To my surprise, working actually helped dull my pain a bit.

One day, after an especially long and stressful day at work, I couldn't wait to get inside my apartment, lie down on my couch, and give in to the tears. I was filled with hopelessness, fear of the future, and a little panic over how I would manage on my own.

As I came up the stairs to my third floor apartment, I gasped. There, on my dark brown doormat, was a white feather.

How did the feather get inside the apartment building?

This was not a breezeway building, but an apartment building with a front door. My whole body shaking, I picked up the white feather and barely managed to open my front door. I still cried my heart out as I entered the apartment that evening, but the white feather confirmed that somebody was actually looking out for me and letting me know that I would be okay.

– Karin Krafft–

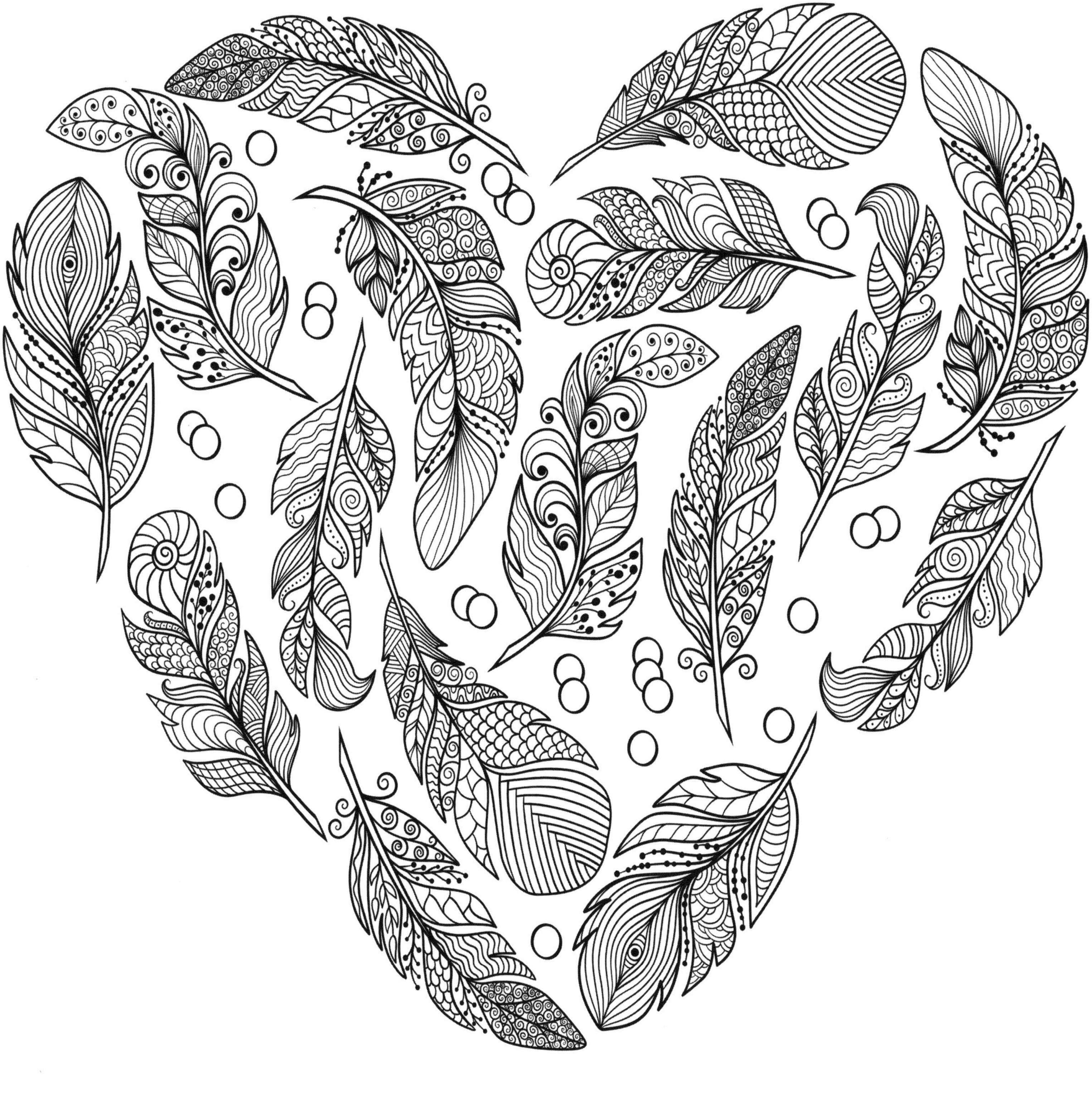

A Special Message

Angels can fly directly into the heart of the matter.
~Author Unknown

My father's surgery would begin in two hours. His health situation – long marred by high blood pressure – had very quickly advanced from problematic to urgent when an ultrasound revealed ninety-nine percent blockage of his carotid and femoral arteries. His cardiologist was amazed that my dad had not already suffered a massive stroke, and surgery had been scheduled so quickly that I could not make it home to Texas in time from the East Coast.

I needed to put on a brave face for my daughter, Brinnley, who was four years old. Brinnley and my dad had a very special relationship. To say that Brinnley loved her "Pop" would be the greatest understatement of all time. Because of it, I had not spoken of his health issues. But as I proceeded to go about our normal morning routine, I noticed that Brinnley was being unusually quiet. I grabbed a cup of coffee and looked over at her.

"Brinnley, are you okay honey?" I asked gently.

Brinnley did not reply. She looked at me, then walked out of the kitchen and headed toward the living room.

My husband, who was frantically getting ready to leave for work, called over to her, "Good morning, Monkey!"

Again, Brinnley acted as though she hadn't heard us. My husband and I looked at each other quizzically and asked, "What's that about?"

Both of us followed her into the living room where we found her at the coffee table. She had gotten her notebook and crayons and begun drawing a picture. We sat down on the couch and attempted to speak to her, but she continued to draw the picture in silence. She seemed so different this morning, not her usual bubbly, chatty self. Instead, she was so focused on her work that it was as if she were in a trance, coloring feverishly to finish by a certain time.

When she finished, she dropped the crayon and stared at the picture. Then she picked up her notebook and walked over to me. "Mommy, this is for you."

I couldn't breathe when I looked at the picture. It was the human heart, perfectly sketched in bright Crayola colors to include chambers and arteries. It was unmistakable.

I took a deep breath and looked into Brinnley's eyes. She was smiling, her beautiful blue eyes locked onto mine.

"Brinnley, what is this?"

Still locked on my gaze, she replied, "Pop is going to be fine, Mommy." And just like that, she turned and walked away, as tears began to stream down my face.

My husband, who had not yet seen the picture asked, "What's wrong?" I handed the picture to him and heard him whisper, "Oh my God," as he placed his hand on mine.

To this day, I don't know how to explain the picture, or how Brinnley knew that my dad would be okay, other than to recognize I observed something extraordinary. After all, she was only four years old... how could she possibly know how to draw something as complex as a human heart with such amazing detail?

I learned later there had been major complications during the surgery, and my father had almost lost his life. It wasn't until a few days later, when I was able to speak to him briefly that he said one thing, "Give a hug and kiss to my angel Brinnley." I felt only then that I truly understood what happened. I am certain it's a miracle that my dad survived and, even more, that my daughter was able to get his message to me when I needed it most.

–Jolie Lisenby–

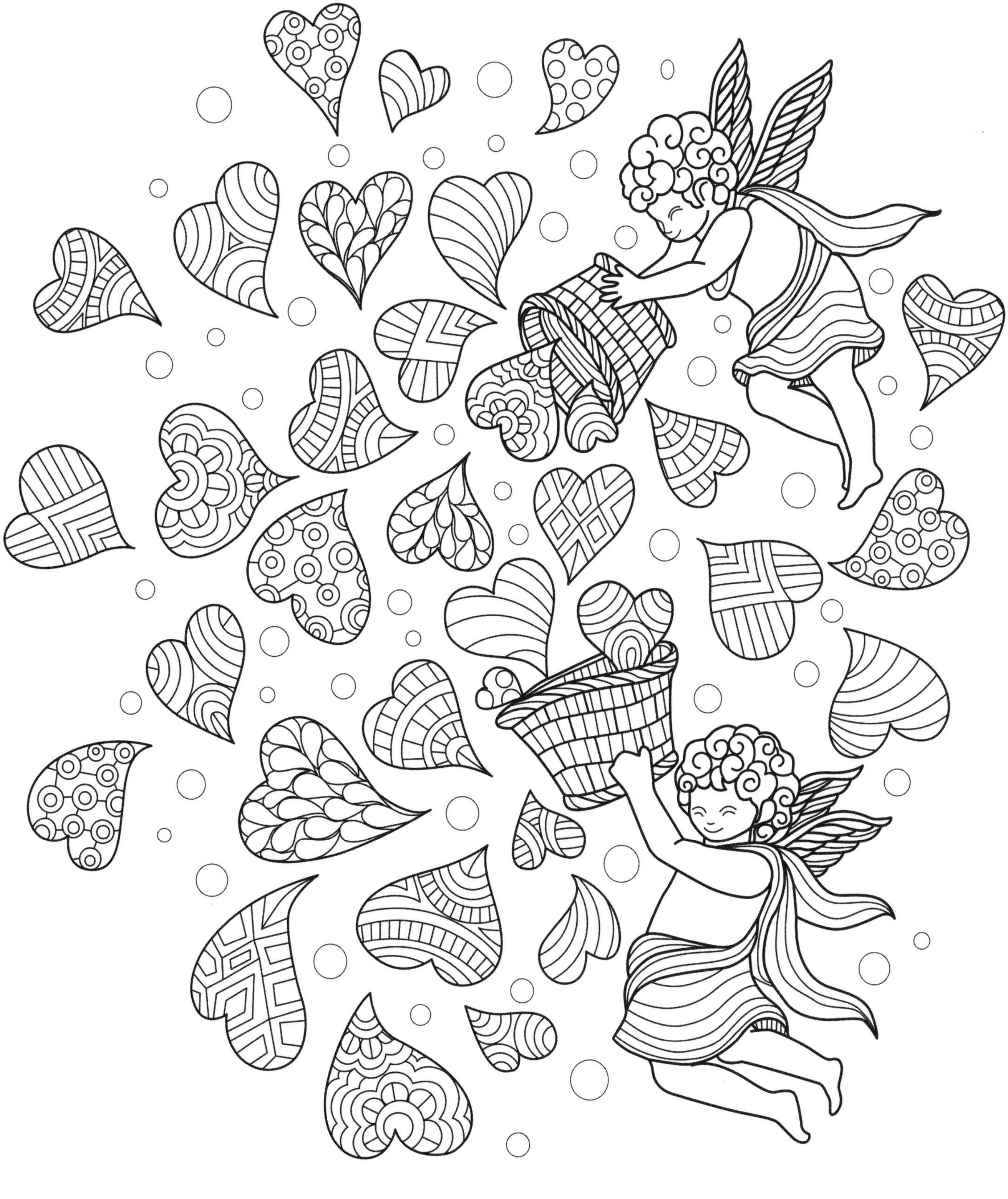

"There really isn't an explanation, unless..."
"Unless what?"
"I think we met an angel," I mumbled.

Excerpt from "Embassy Miracle" by Barbara S. Canale, a story in *Chicken Soup for the Soul: Angels & Miracles*

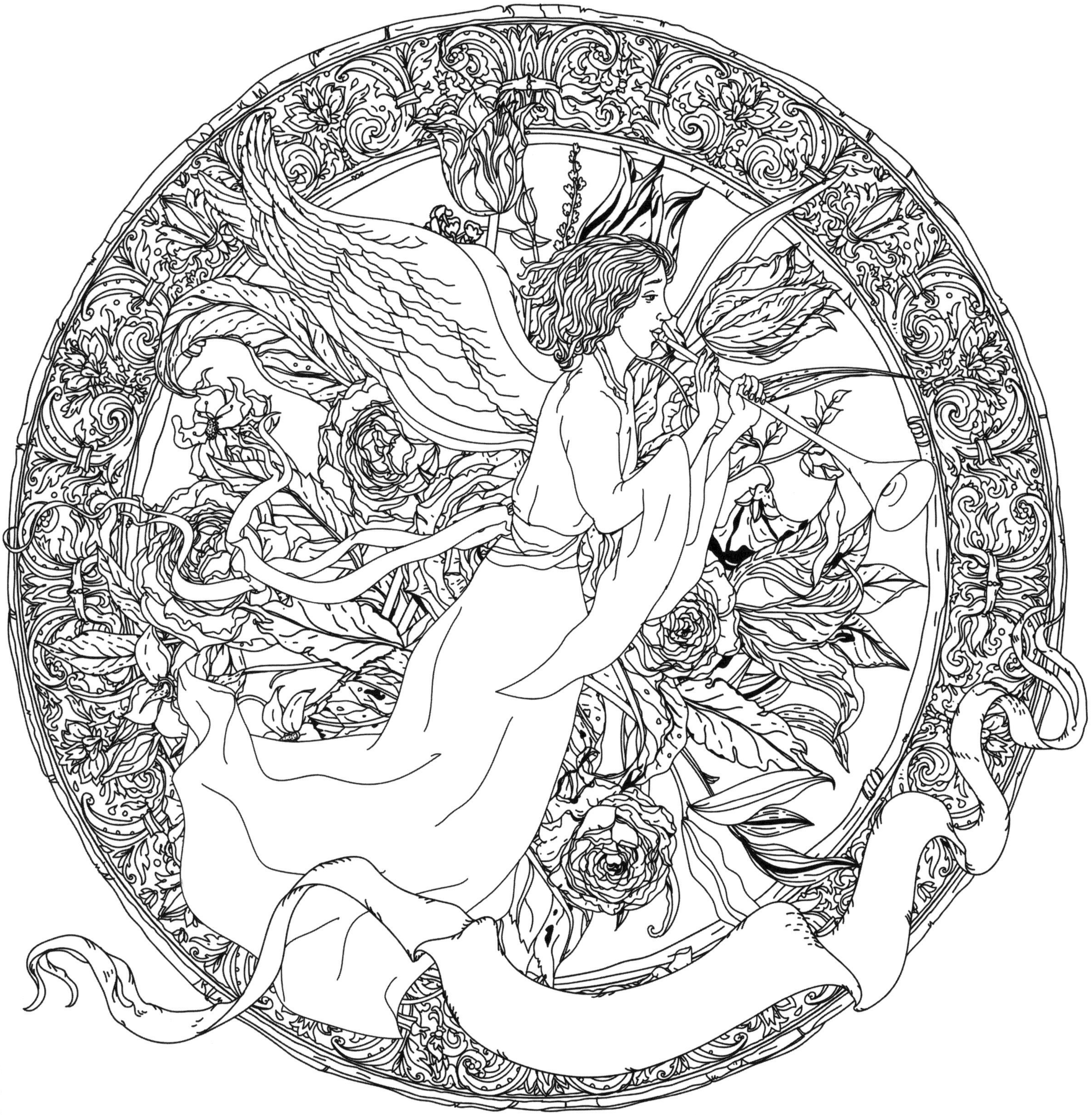

Ask and You Shall Receive

*Prayer at its highest is a two-way conversation and for me
the most important part is listening to God's replies.*
~Frank C. Laubach

I was planting flowers one May, and watching our four-year-old son ride his bicycle on our farm by himself. I worried that he would always be playing alone with no siblings by his side. My husband and I endured years of infertility treatments before realizing that God's plan for us was adoption. We adopted our first son as a newborn, and he was a dream come true! But, we had always hoped for a house full of children.

When our son was two, we updated our paperwork and put our names back in the waiting "pool" along with hundreds of other couples hoping to adopt a child. I prayed daily that God would add to our family. But, I was becoming impatient and even our son was starting to question the wait.

"Mom, when do you think I will have a little brother or sister?" he asked that evening. With sadness and frustration in my heart, I replied, "You will have to ask God about that."

Later that night, my husband arrived home, and I told him about our son's questions and my response to him.

So, he asked our son if he had asked God.

"Yes!" our son replied. "He said it would be on Thursday."

I tucked our son in that Monday night and quickly forgot about his divine prediction.

A few days later, I was busy preparing supper when the phone rang. I vaguely recognized the name on the caller ID. Where had I seen that name before?

"Is your husband home, too?" the pleasant voice on the line asked. "Can you call him to the phone? I have some exciting news to share," she said.

It wasn't registering yet, but I hollered for my husband to come to the phone. I was on the phone in the kitchen, and my husband picked up the phone in the office a few rooms away.

The call was from our adoption agency. The caseworker was calling to tell us that a baby boy was born on Monday – the same day my son sent up his prayers. The baby boy's birth parents had decided on an adoption plan and picked us to be the adoptive parents!

I couldn't see my husband, but I could tell by his trembling voice that he was starting to cry.

"It's Thursday," he said, choking back tears of joy. He had remembered our son's prayer.

My knees went weak, and I almost fell to the floor. Just as God had told my son. It was Thursday, and this one phone call was about to change our lives forever.

The birth parents wanted to meet us the next day! I'm a planner who doesn't generally like surprises, so this was extremely stressful but in the best way possible.

We drove to meet the birth parents three hours away on Friday. By Saturday, we were a family of four!

And, God had even more surprises for us that year as He decided to add to our family again just eleven months later by sending us a daughter, too.

—Kristine Jacobson—

God Laughs

The most beautiful thing we can experience is the mysterious.
~Albert Einstein

One of the most astounding occurrences that I've ever witnessed at my church happened when I was hosting a group from out of town. The group included Jean, Lynette, and Audrey.

When Sunday came they decided to go to my church. It was an ecumenical group. Jean was a Roman Catholic, Audrey was a Quaker, Lynette did not attend church, and I was a Presbyterian.

As we went into the church, Lynette commented "I haven't set foot in a church for over thirty years. The ceiling will probably come down."

I almost always sit in the back row, but they marched in and sat right in the front row so I joined them there. We had just settled into our seats when we heard a loud crash. A chunk of one of the ceiling lamps fell down right in front of Lynette. Never before in the more than fifty years I have attended that church had such a thing happened. Furthermore, there are about thirty seats in the front row, yet the chunk fell directly in front of Lynette.

Although I am a medical doctor, I do like numbers. My undergraduate major in college was biostatistics. Probability is of special interest to me. The probability of our sitting in the front row is fairly small. The probability of a piece of a light fixture falling when one had not fallen in the previous fifty-plus years is extremely small. The probability of that piece falling in front of our row and in front of Lynette, the person who made the joke, and right after we sat down, is infinitesimally small.

Coincidence or the hand of God, you'll have to make up your own mind. If it is the hand of God, He surely has a sense of humor. Maybe He was sending a message to Lynette: "If this is what it takes to make you believe, I will do it."

–Doris V. Schoon–

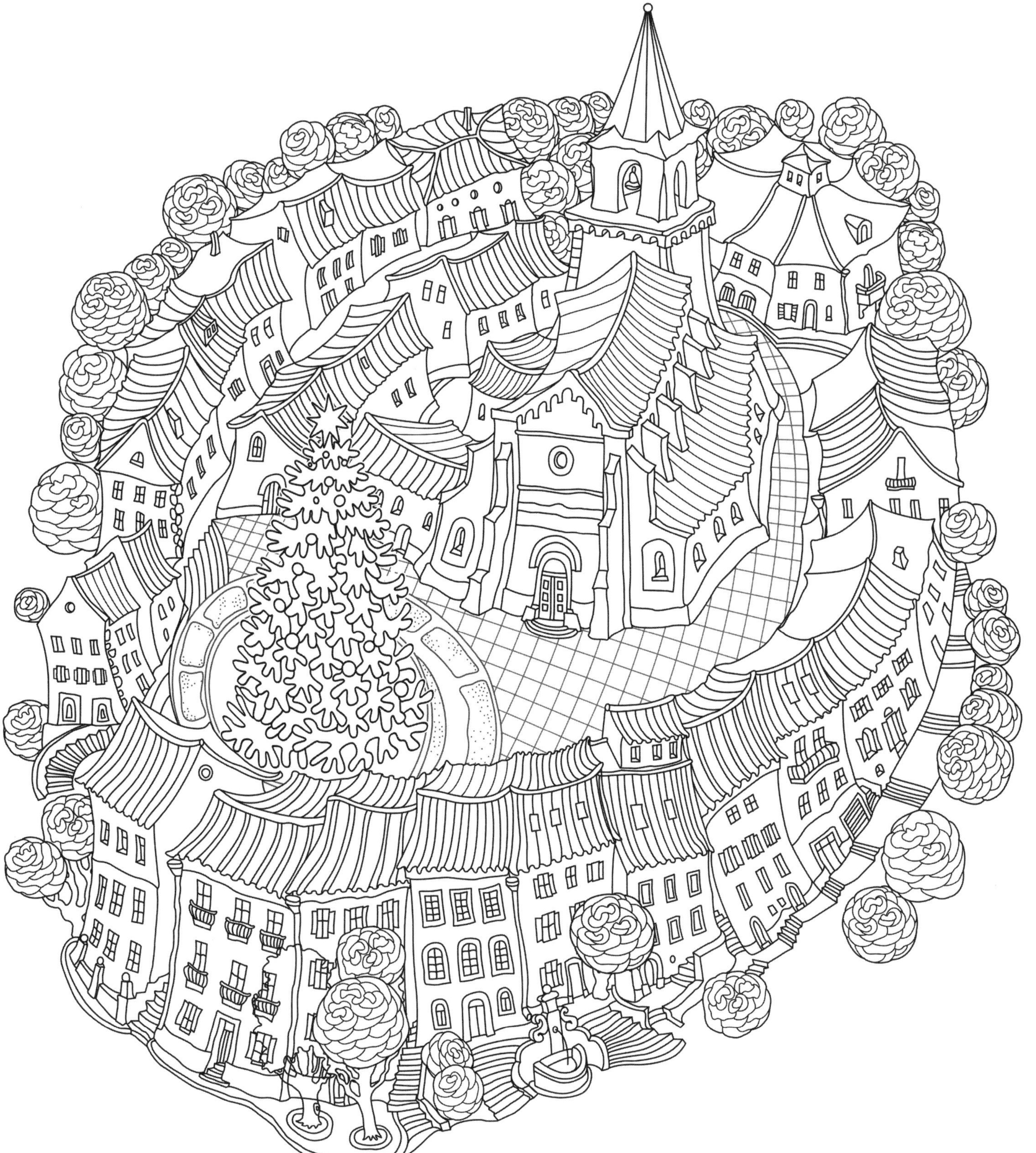

A Voice in the Desert

*Angels deliver Fate to our doorstep – and
anywhere else it is needed.
~Jessi Lane Adams*

I was jogging around our base in Tikrit, Iraq. As I rounded the corner I could see the front gate and was glad the run was almost over. Then, as I headed for the final stretch, a voice in my head said, "Take cover behind the wall."

I looked up and did not see any imminent danger. There were no missiles in the sky, the alarm bell was not sounding, and everything was relatively quiet. I kept jogging, assuming that the paranoia of being on a battlefield had begun to take its toll on me. Then I paused for a moment as I got closer to the wall because my brain was screaming, "Take cover!"

Suddenly, I heard a bloodcurdling scream coming from the front gate. As I whipped my head around I saw a huge ball of flames, and then everything went black. When I woke up I was at the medical station with the medic staring down at me. I was confused about what was going on. The medic told me to hang on a minute and went off. He brought back one of the other medics with whom I had done a great deal of work during my deployment. Jim put his hand on my shoulder and said, "Ma'am, you were the only survivor. Do you remember anything that happened?"

I was stunned and couldn't speak. Jim told the others that I might be in shock. I looked at him puzzled and said, "All I remember is screaming, a large bang, and then a fire ball. The fire ball was about a mile across." Jim nodded and said that would make sense because it was a tanker full of explosives that detonated at the gate. I instantly felt sick. I knew there were always six guards stationed at the gate. I asked about them and Jim repeated quietly, "You are the only survivor."

And with that I became consumed with "survivor guilt."

Once released, I went back to my bunk, where I found glass had shattered all over my bed and belongings. My roommates greeted me enthusiastically and asked how I survived. I explained that I had heard a voice telling me to stay behind the wall and so I did though I did not know why. My closest friend, Kathy, said quite simply, "Well, you have a divine purpose; that much is for sure." I doubted her. After all I was a single person with no real purpose in life, so that could not be the case.

A few weeks later, I received an e-mail from Robin, the mother of a girl named Erica who I had been a "big sister" to for the past six years. Its message was simple:

"Linda, Child Protective Services took Marissa. Can you please get her back when you come home?"

Marissa was Robin's grandchild and Erica's niece. I knew her and had taken care of her on many occasions prior to my deployment. I was confused, though. I was a "big sister," a volunteer, not an official foster parent. When I went back to my bunk I sat staring off into space. Kathy came over to me and said, "What's up you?"

I told her about the e-mail I had received. Kathy and I had been friends for years, so she had met Erica and Marissa. She gripped my shoulder and stared at me intently. "Linda, don't you see? You survived the explosion to be a mother!" I shook my head in disagreement; after all foster care is temporary. But Kathy shook her head firmly and said, "No your purpose is to be Marissa's mother."

When I returned home I did in fact go through the steps to gain custody of Marissa. I learned she had a sister, Mary, who no one had mentioned, so I took her, too. After fostering them for two years, I adopted Marissa and Mary.

Kathy was right. That voice saved me for a very special purpose, to be a mom to two wonderful young girls.

– L. Thorburn–

"You have a divine purpose; that much is for sure."

The Teddy Bear

Earl's crossed arms and permanent grimace told everyone in the room he didn't want to be there. Meanwhile, Kim wiped away tears as she expressed her desire for a happy marriage with a husband who managed his anger.

The couple was attending a Cleansing Stream seminar, led by Church on the Way in Van Nuys, California. Earl, sporting a two-day stubble on his chin, was a bear of a guy – an angry, burly man with an intimidating scowl. Kim, on the other hand, radiated warmth and faith.

During a portion of the seminar held at a hotel, Earl and Kim joined three other couples for informal counseling and prayer. I was part of the Cleansing Stream's leadership team and I began with routine questions: "Where did you meet? How long have you been married? What do you do for a living?"

Earl grunted a few answers between complaints about this "inquisition," but I could see right through his bravado. Something was bothering him.

Kim said that if Earl didn't get help soon, the marriage would be over. Years of belligerence and shouting had taken their toll.

The session concluded with a time of prayer. With my eyes closed, I kept seeing a fuzzy brown teddy bear with a plaid bow around its neck. I wondered if I hadn't gotten enough sleep the previous night. What did a teddy bear have to do with this guy and his deep-rooted anger?

As the meeting broke for lunch, a leader asked if Earl felt any differently. "I never believed in any of this prayer stuff anyway, so the answer is no," he replied. "I only did this for my wife."

I leaned over to my husband and said, "I know this sounds crazy, but the Lord wants me to buy Earl a teddy bear."

My husband rolled his eyes, but after twenty-nine years of marriage, he had learned that my spiritual antennae usually picked up the right signals. "Okay, let's go find one."

At a nearby market, which happened to be having a sale on teddy bears, I found the exact bear I envisioned: a furry brown bear with a plaid bow around its neck. I purchased the bear and found a gift card too. I wrote a note explaining that God had told me to give Earl the bear, although I didn't know why.

When the seminar regrouped in the hotel ballroom, I found Earl and Kim sitting toward the back. I walked over and handed Earl the brown paper bag holding the bear and card. When he lifted the bear out of the bag, Earl clutched it to his chest and his shoulders began heaving uncontrollably. Tears rolled down his cheeks. People couldn't help looking his way.

After pulling him aside for a few minutes, the seminar leaders asked Earl to approach the podium in the front of the room. He did, clutching Kim and his teddy bear.

"I would like to thank the group for praying for me today," he stammered. "Something happened here today, and it happened because a lady bought me this teddy bear. You see, no one in the whole world knows what this teddy bear means to me. When I was a little boy, I had a very cruel father who regularly beat me. One day I disobeyed him and, for my punishment, he took my favorite teddy bear to the back yard incinerator, where he burned it right before my eyes. I was so crushed, so hurt, that I never forgave him. I realize today that God knew my unforgiveness caused great anger in my marriage. Now that God gave me back my teddy bear, I can start healing."

Dabbing at my tears, I sat in awe of God's tender grace and unfailing love.

–Judith Ann Hayes–

All in Good Time

Time is a physician that heals every grief.
~Diphilus

After my father was gone I visited Mom more frequently. Eventually we began sorting through Daddy's belongings and Mom gave me his watch.

"You take this, Annie. I know you will appreciate having it someday."

She placed the watch in my hand and my fingers closed around it. I recalled him slipping the watch over his calloused hand every morning as he descended the stairs to start his day.

"Thanks, Mom," I said, trying not to cry.

I put that big watch on my wrist even though its large face and its extra wide band looked comical on me. I didn't care. My father wore it every day and I resolved that I'd wear it every day, too. And there it stayed no matter the occasion. When I went to bed I'd slide my arm under the pillow and listen to the rhythmic tick, tick, tick that eventually lulled me to sleep.

On the first anniversary of Dad's passing, I noticed the watch had stopped at the exact time of his death – 5:17 p.m. It occurred to me that this might be Dad's way of telling me it was time to move on. I put the watch in my jewelry box.

During that second year after his death, I helped my mother downsize. She gave away or sold most of her furniture, readied the house for sale, and found a new place to live in a retirement community. Even though she would be without Dad, Mom was looking forward to making new friends in the retirement community.

I didn't realize it at first, but slowly the cloud of grief was lifting from my heart, too. Mom and I would often end up in a fit of laughter recalling one incident or another with my father. Still, I wanted answers. I needed to know he was happy even though he'd moved on. I prayed often for his peace and happiness but accepted that I'd never know for sure.

Mom was well settled into her new life and carrying on as best she could when we neared the second anniversary of Dad's departure. I hadn't thought of the watch in months. Then, one day, I came across it in my jewelry box. I picked it up and discovered to my astonishment that not only was it running, but it was also showing the correct time and date. How could that be? It had stopped cold right on the very first anniversary of his death. I'd looked at it a few times since it had initially stopped and the time and date had never changed. Yet now it was keeping perfect time.

Dad's watch continued to run perfectly, never losing a minute, for the next ten years. Watch batteries just don't have that kind of longevity.

When that watch came roaring back to life long after it had stopped, Daddy was letting me know loud and clear, "Don't worry about me, Annie, I couldn't be happier." Of this I have no doubt.

—Annmarie B. Tait—

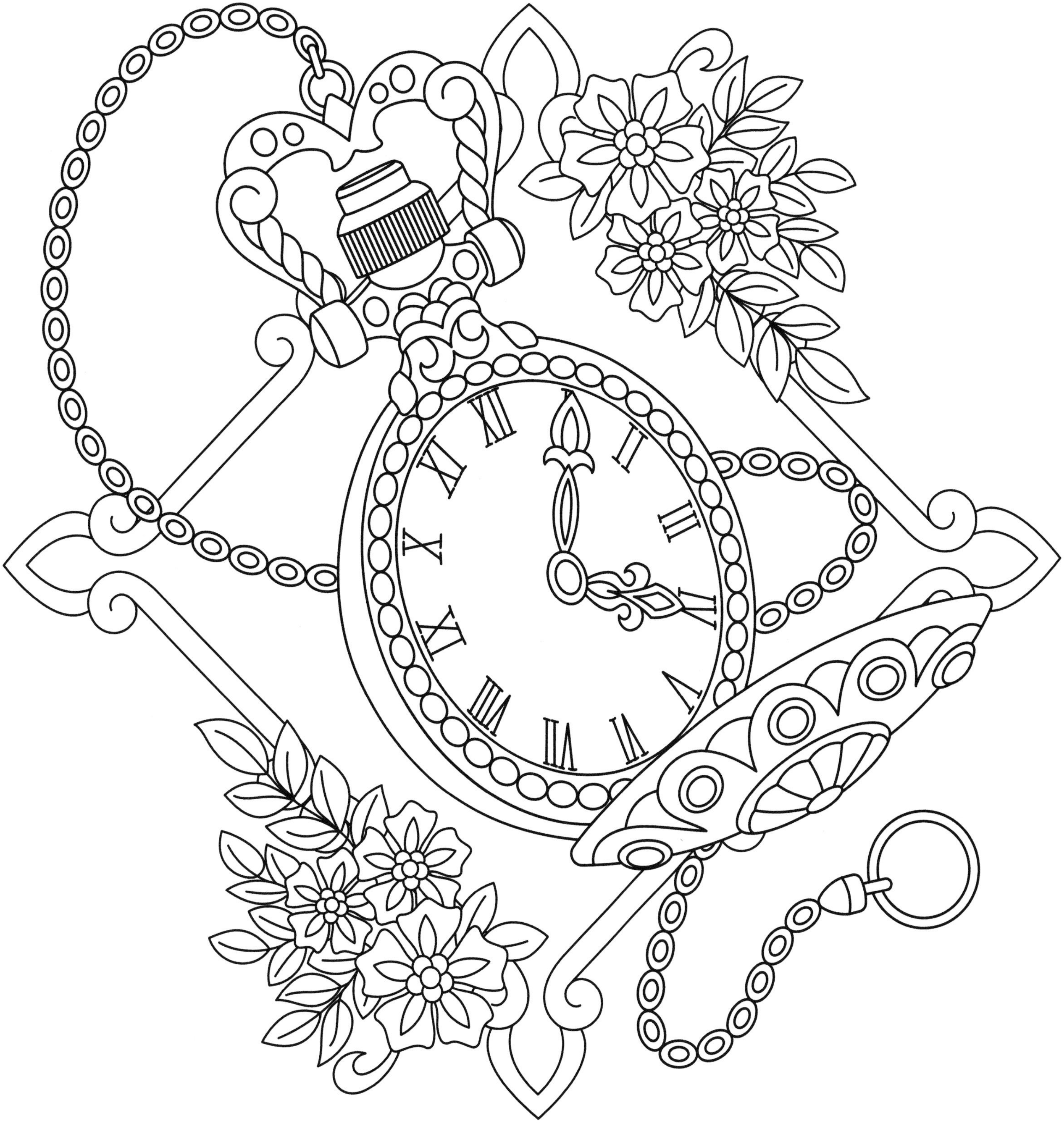

Christmas Comfort

Grandmas hold our tiny hands for just a little
while, but our hearts forever.
~Author Unknown

My mother had passed away in October and I was bereft. Our fifteen-year-old daughter Jessica was despondent, too. Her Mimi had been her world.

We had run away to out-of-town relatives for Thanksgiving, and now we faced our first Christmas without my mother. To make it more painful, Jess's birthday was Christmas Eve. My husband suggested we escape to New York. What could be more festive than the holiday lights and Broadway shows?

We had gone to the theatre that night, had enjoyed a late supper afterward, and had returned to the hotel exhausted. Our room had a wonderfully inviting king size bed, which the three of us shared. Robert fell onto his side and was deep into dreams before Jess and I had washed our faces. I crawled into the middle with Jess to my right. She had been unusually quiet and I knew she was missing her grandmother when I heard her whisper, "Mom, would you please 'tickle-scratch' my back?"

"Sure, sweetheart." My mother had been the world's best backscratcher. She had the lightest touch and the greatest endurance anyone could ever imagine. How many nights had that gentle hand lulled me to sleep, her fingers barely sweeping over my skin from shoulder to shoulder and across my neck? Unfortunately for Jess, I had inherited neither the instinct nor the patience to do it the way Mama had done. But I would try.

Jess turned her back to me, and, as I lifted my arm toward her shoulder, the atmosphere in the room seemed to change. It became cooler – not unpleasantly so, but cooler and different. Where it had been completely dark the minute before, there was now a soft glow around us, and then, something, or someone, took my hand and guided it over and around my daughter's back. It was as if my hand had become the object on a Ouija board. I did nothing. My delicate movements were totally involuntary and foreign to me. My own hand was weightless and tireless. I had no control over where or how to touch her – or when to stop. Eventually, my hand moved to the top of her left shoulder and patted it twice. With that, the session ended, and the darkness returned.

I brought my hand back to myself and pondered what had just transpired. A few moments later, I thought I heard Jess sniffle.

"Are you still awake, honey?"

"Uh huh. Mom, Mimi was here, wasn't she?"

"It seemed that way. Why do you say so?"

"Somehow the room felt different, strange. And the way you scratched me felt just like her. You never have done it for so long. And then the signal that you were through."

"Signal?"

"You tapped me twice on the shoulder. That's what she always did when she was finished."

"I don't remember her doing that. Hmm, I guess that really was Mimi letting us know she is still with us and she is okay." With that Jess hugged me and fell fast asleep.

We could not have had a better Christmas present.

–Grace Givens–

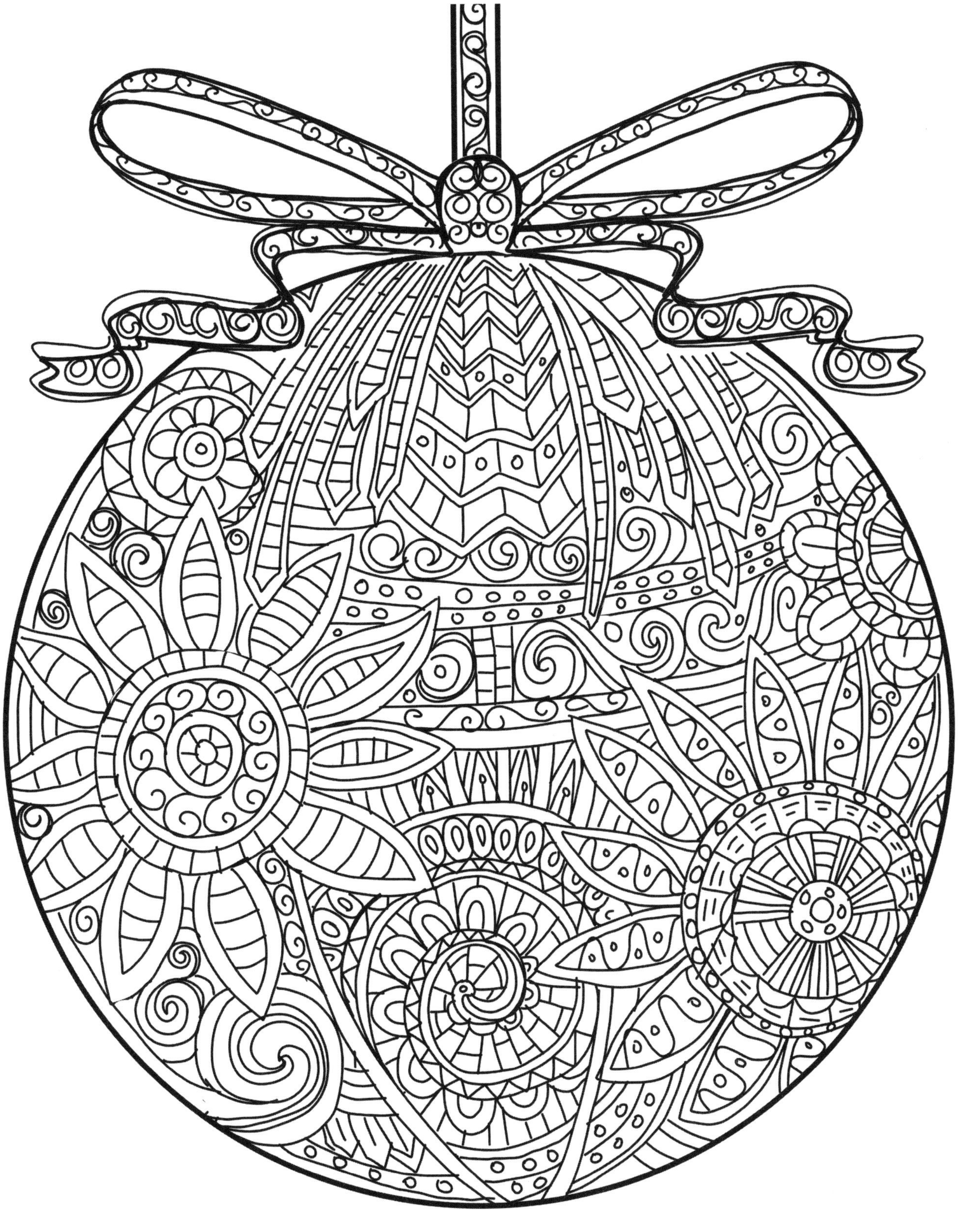

Double Exposure

A mother's love runs deep and its
power knows no limit.
~Author Unknown

The last time my mother was at our house was Thanksgiving Day. She had been diagnosed with advanced stage cancer two months earlier, and she was already showing signs of weakness. So instead of the usual "Thanksgiving at Grandma's house," we decided to have it at ours.

By the time everyone arrived, the house smelled of turkey and stuffing, and the tables looked festive and inviting. It was a good day for my mom and dad, with a house full of children and grandchildren. We ate and laughed about times growing up. Then, while the kids played, we put the football game on TV and played pinochle with my dad.

It was nice for us to see my mom dressed up and out of their house for a change. She spent most of that day sitting in the comfortable rocker in the living room. We took lots of pictures that Thanksgiving.

After that day, Mom's condition worsened quickly. She died two weeks later, just before Christmas. It was the first of many holidays and special occasions without Mom there to celebrate with us.

Time lessened the grief, but we still missed her very much. She and my dad had always been there for their grandchildren's birthdays, school events and special times in their lives, and my dad still came. One of those special occasions arrived the following spring.

Our youngest daughter made her First Holy Communion, which is a special celebration in our church. I got out the white dress and veil that my mother had bought for me when I made my First Communion. I washed it and hung it out to dry. The lace sparkled in the sun. I replaced the yellowed ribbon and sewed a new white slip. How sad, I thought, that Mom would not be here to see her granddaughter on this day. Sarah was especially close to her grandma and grandpa. She had spent a lot of time with them before she started school, since they babysat her when I returned to work. It would be the only First Communion of our six children that my mom would miss.

We had lots of family over that day and, as usual, we took lots of pictures with family and friends. I was anxious to see the pictures, and quickly took them in to be developed. This was back before digital cameras, when you had to load the film into the camera, and then take the film to the drugstore to have the pictures developed.

When I picked up the photos I opened the folder, and for a moment my heart almost stopped. Right on top was a picture of Sarah in her communion dress sitting on the arm of the rocker, and next to her, sitting in that comfortable rocker, was my mother! The picture was a little fuzzy, but there was no mistake – it was Sarah and her grandma, on the day that she made her First Communion.

When I got over my initial shock and looked through the rest of the pictures, I realized that the photos had been double-exposed – communion pictures taken on top of Thanksgiving pictures. In the time that had passed there were holidays and birthdays when I had taken other pictures. But somehow I had missed taking in this one roll of film from Thanksgiving. And I had re-used that roll of undeveloped film on that day, thinking it was a new roll of film.

What were the odds! But that day in May, my daughter's picture was taken sitting next to her grandma. It was as if my mother was sending a message from heaven saying, "See, I haven't missed anything! I've been right here beside you all the time."

—Peggy Archer—

Maybe it was a visitation, a smile from Kevin who had been a sweet, happy, and extremely friendly young man. Perhaps it was his way of saying, "I'm okay! It's beautiful here on the other side. Don't worry about me." The miracle of a rainbow as a Mother's Day gift was perfect.

Excerpt from "Rainbow Story" by Lava Mueller, a story in *Chicken Soup for the Soul: Angels & Miracles*

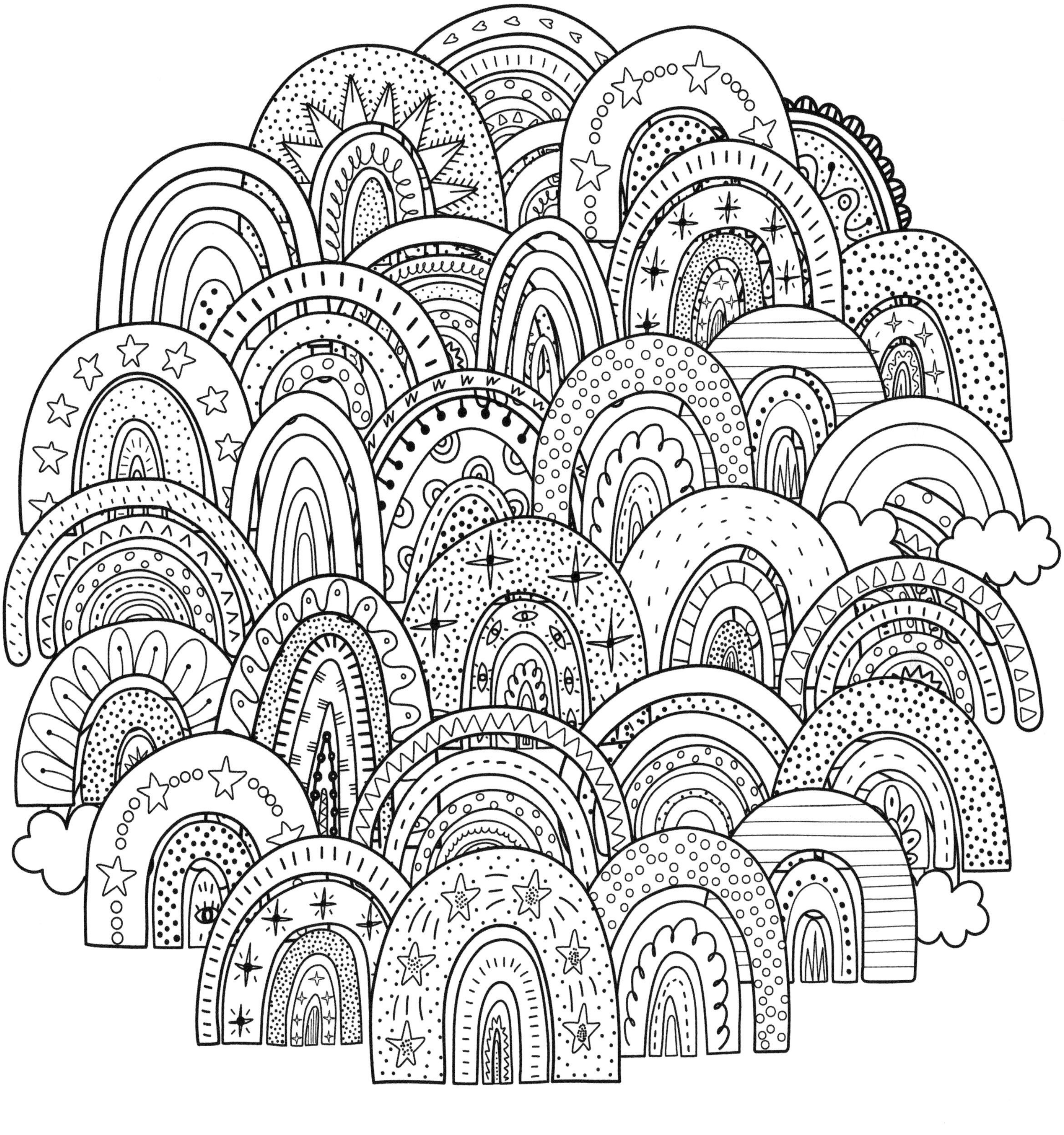

Did You Love Me?

My soul ached. I stared blankly at the e-mail I had received telling me my husband had succumbed to ALS. It had been ten long months since his sudden departure a few weeks after our wedding. He couldn't put me through it, he said. He couldn't watch *me* watch *him* dwindle to nothingness.

The last time we spoke he told me that when the time came, I should go to our favorite beach and celebrate him.

The coolness of the California night hit me immediately as I pulled into the hotel. The sadness of his death coupled with the last ten grueling months weighed heavy on me. I slept deeply and woke at the crack of dawn with only one thought fueling me: "Get to the beach." I quickly dressed in my running clothes and jumped into my truck. I drove the few short miles to our favorite beach and parked, inhaling the delicious salt air and letting the gentle sound of the pounding waves soothe me.

What had bothered me during those ten months was simple: How had I married someone who could leave me so easily? Did he love me? Did I not know what love was? How could I be so blind? Why did God let this happen?

I felt used and foolish. Our courtship and wedding had been beautiful. Despite the fact that he was dying, we felt like we had it all. We truly felt God had a greater purpose for us and would see us through what was going to be a difficult time.

I remembered the laughter, the inside jokes, his love of Coca-Cola and the half empty Coke cans he would leave in the fridge. I thought about the way he would look at me and brag about me to anyone who would listen.

And then he was gone and I was alone, left to wonder what had just happened.

As I made my way from the cliff to the beach below, I was alone. The surfers were still up top staring at the waves. It was overcast and as I started to run I noticed how smooth and blank the wet sand was, the tide having just gone out. Suddenly I was sprinting, my heart beating hard and my breath catching in the cool morning air. I ran and ran until I couldn't hold back the tears any longer.

I stopped running and faced the ocean, shouting my anguish to the Lord.

"Why did this happen? I thought You had a purpose for us! Why did he leave? Did he ever love me?" I sat down in the still wet sand and sobbed.

And then I heard a voice. "Look at where you came from..."

I sniffed loudly and ran my arm under my runny nose. "Look at where I came from?" I answered angrily, "That's all I've been doing!"

The voice was still and small. "Look at where you came from..."

I sniffed again, got up, and dutifully looked at where I had come from on the beach and gasped, my hand flying to my mouth.

There was another set of shoe prints right next to mine in the wet sand. I looked around. Could I have missed seeing someone else on the beach? No, I was still alone.

Excitement rose in me, "Lord! Is it You?" I asked. "No, it can't be You. You'd be barefoot!" I exclaimed.

I bent over the prints and looked at the familiar running shoe tread of my husband's shoes in the sand next to mine, his stride longer than mine, but there! Once ALS had taken his hands, I had put those shoes on his feet so many times that I knew the tread like the back of my own hand.

I started to cry again, but this time they were tears of joy. My words were a jumble talking to him and to God.

"You did love me, you did, thank you," I sang out through the tears. "Thank you Lord for letting me know. Thank you for healing me. Thank you for this confirmation, and look Jon, your foot isn't dragging! It must feel so good for you to run! ALS can't touch you in Heaven!"

–Lily Blais–

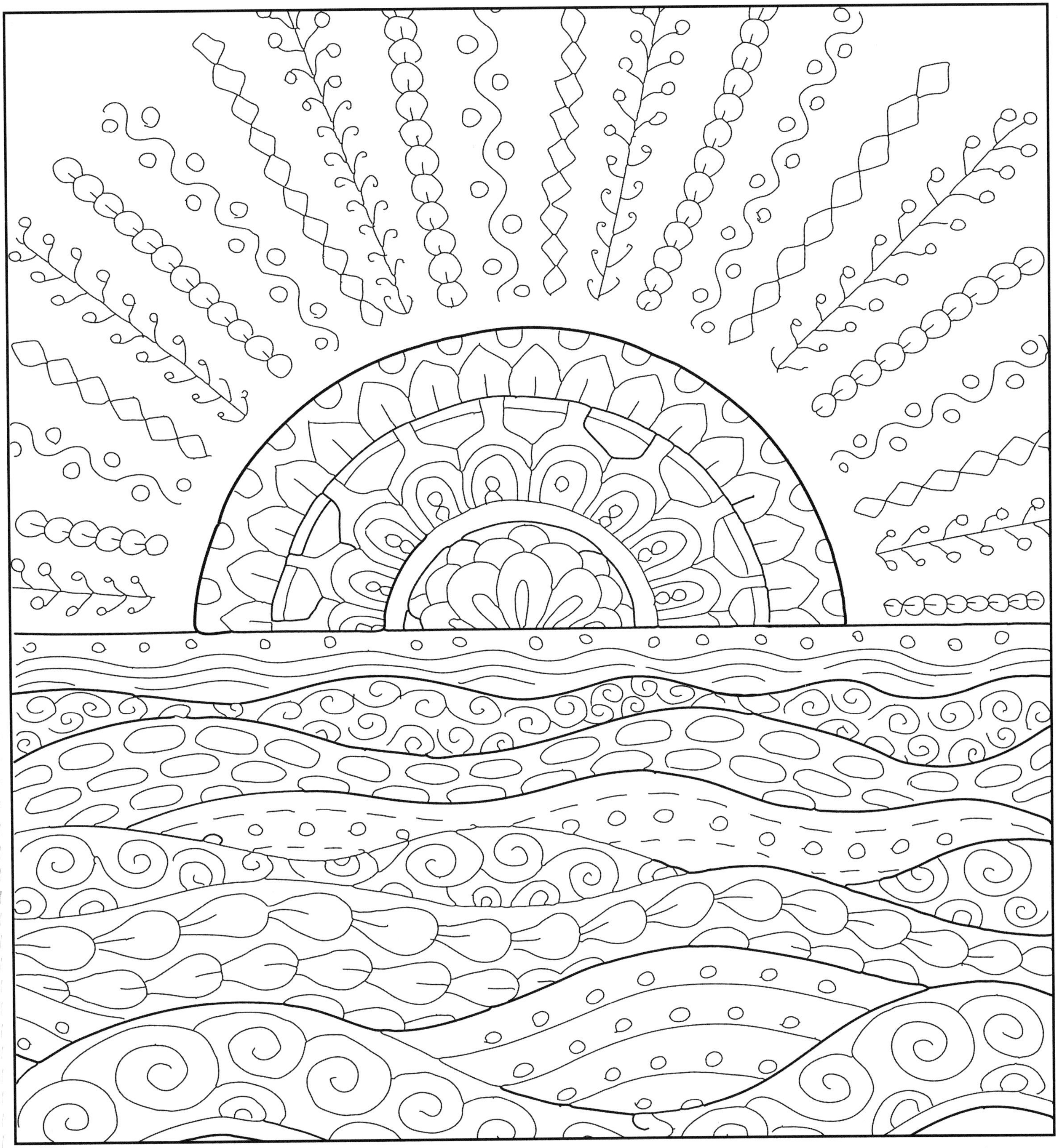

I know that each of us is supposed to have a guardian angel, and I believe mine came to my rescue that night. For me, it's the only conclusion that makes any sense.

Excerpt from "A Desperate Situation" by Connie Kutac, a story in *Chicken Soup for the Soul: Angels & Miracles*

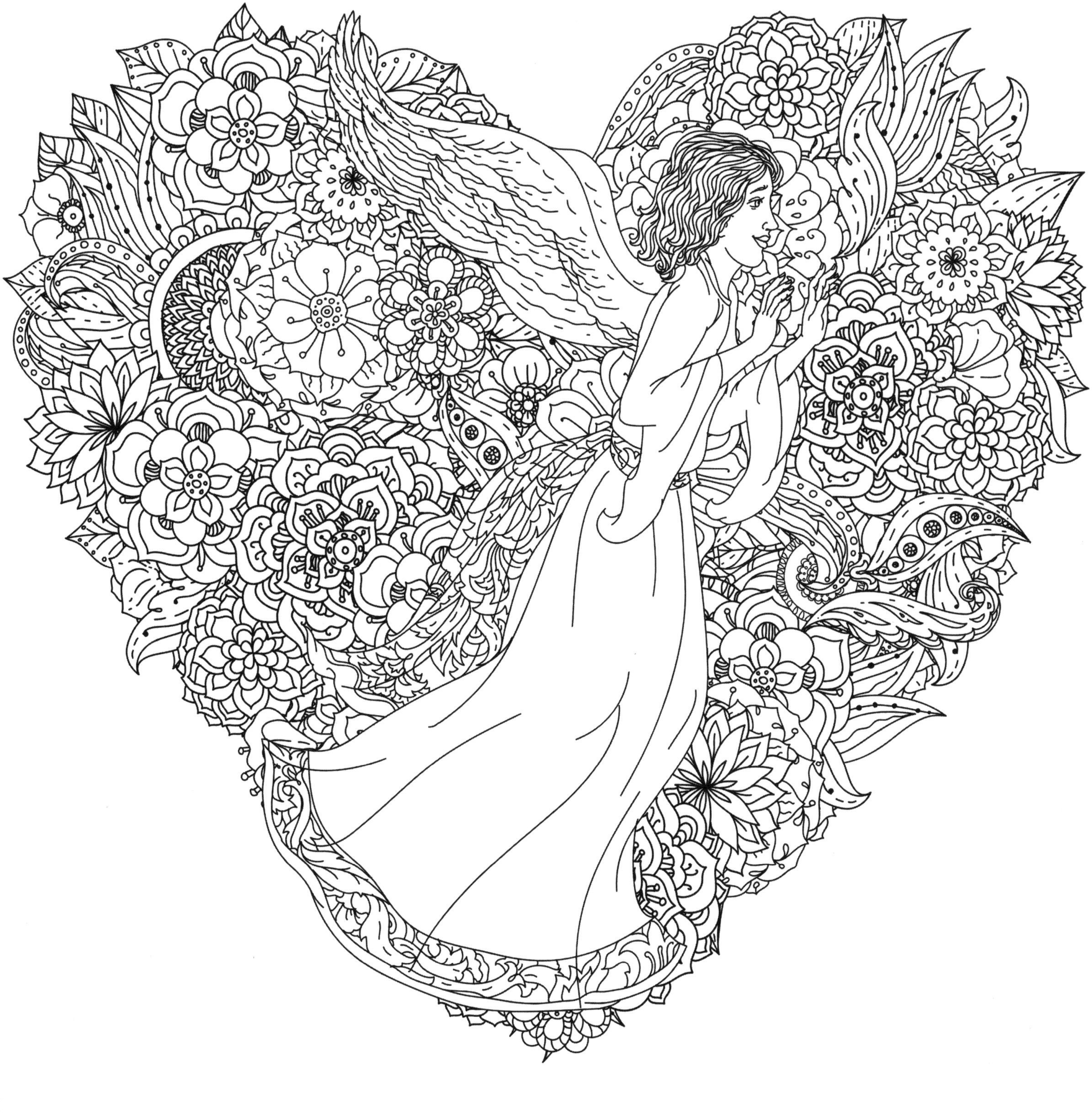

Courtesy of iStockphoto.com (©mashabr)

A Thousand Cranes of Hope

Cranes carry this heavy mystical baggage. They're icons of fidelity and happiness. The Vietnamese believe cranes cart our souls up to heaven on their wings.
~Mitchell Burgess

A visit to the hospital is rarely a pleasant one. Its distinctive smell of disinfectant is never welcoming to the senses. Its white walls with the occasional splash of colour – seemingly an attempt to lift the spirits of the crestfallen souls that enter – is never encouraging enough.

As I made my way to the ward, I took a deep breath and practised a smile. After all, nobody needed another miserable face in the room.

As I entered the ward, I overheard my relatives making plans for a funeral. My grandfather had been in a coma for almost a week, with a discouraging diagnosis from the doctor. "It's only wise to make plans now," my uncle said.

I wondered. Was this really the end for him?

My grandfather was a distant figure in the family. A man of very few words, his stern demeanour made him seem unapproachable.

However, I saw him in a different light. Raised at my grandparents' place since young, I forged a very close relationship with them. While my grandmother played the role of bad cop, my grandfather and I were partners in crime. He would sneak me downstairs for ice cream when Grandmother was in the bathroom, while I secretly added more sugar in his morning drink because he had a sweet tooth that Grandmother disapproved of.

But as I grew older and moved back in with my parents, Grandfather returned to being the quiet and lonely man everyone else saw.

I wanted to awaken this quiet man. I did not believe it was his time to go.

I had an idea. I had read about paper cranes and wishes coming true. For every one thousand folded origami cranes, we get a wish granted by the gods. Absurd as it sounds to the adults, I managed to convince my sisters and cousin to carry out this sacred plan. My family believed in Buddhism, while my cousin's family believed in Christianity. We therefore believed that with combined powers, any wish would come true. We had to act fast so that before death could claim him, God would save him.

In between classes, I was folding origami cranes. Before bedtime, I placed them all in a jar. Watching the jar fill up day by day was akin to filling up the hope in our hearts. Every origami crane was accompanied by a little prayer that my grandfather would open his eyes to see the world again.

The last few cranes were completed at the hospital. We left the jars of origami cranes by his bed and said a final prayer. This was it. Would God save him?

A week later, he was still in a deep sleep. That night, I bawled my eyes out lamenting the gods for not granting our wish. The one thousand origami cranes had not delivered our wish to the gods. We only had one wish – was that too much to ask for?

Just when all hope seemed lost, a call from my aunt one afternoon changed everything. She wanted us to come to the hospital immediately – my grandfather was awake.

A visit to the hospital is rarely a pleasant one. However, this time, I was greeted by the scent of flowers that visitors brought, and thank-you cards from discharged patients pinned on the staff notice board. I stepped into my grandfather's ward and saw him holding our jar of origami cranes. This man of few words looked up at me and said, "My good girl, thank you."

–Pebbles H.–

Three-Dollar Miracle

We all have a guardian angel, sent down from above.
To keep us safe from harm and
surround us with their love.
~Author Unknown

I braced myself against the biting spring wind as I walked through the pharmacy's sliding doors into the parking lot. I stuffed my empty hands into my coat pockets. They were empty, too. Disgusted, I shook my head. What had my life come to? I didn't even have enough money to refill my prescription. The time had come to admit it. I was broke.

How quickly I had stepped over that line. One day I was holding a paycheck and the next day I was holding a pink slip. Twenty-two years of employment hadn't meant much when my company decided to cut costs. With a mortgage and plenty of other bills to pay, I blew through my savings in no time. Now, here I stood, unable to purchase a simple necessity for the lack of three dollars.

My feet felt leaden and I stood outside that pharmacy for a long time, despite the gusting wind, pondering my dilemma. I felt so desperate, I even entertained the idea of asking the next customer who walked toward the pharmacy for the three dollars I needed.

My late mother would have taken a different tack, I thought, as I stood there contemplating my next move. Mom had long subscribed to the notion that we are each assigned a guardian angel – ready to help out in tough situations, waiting to be asked for assistance. Mom made no apologies to anyone about her firm belief and much to the amusement of many naysayers had actually given her guardian angel a name.

I had been one of those naysayers. Yet at that moment I felt so hopeless, a cry came from deep inside me: "I've tried to do everything right. I worked hard and now I have nothing to show for it. I'm scared. If my guardian angel is really out there," I pled, "please help me." Then I tipped my head down to keep the dust in the air from blowing into my eyes. And right in front of me, three dollar bills floated directly toward my feet.

While my practical side prefers to maintain a healthy skepticism about such things, I no longer count myself among the doubters. That experience in a windy parking lot seems like proof positive that I do have a guardian angel. I've been pondering names for her for quite a while now. I'm not sure, but think I'll call her "Mom."

–Monica A. Andermann–

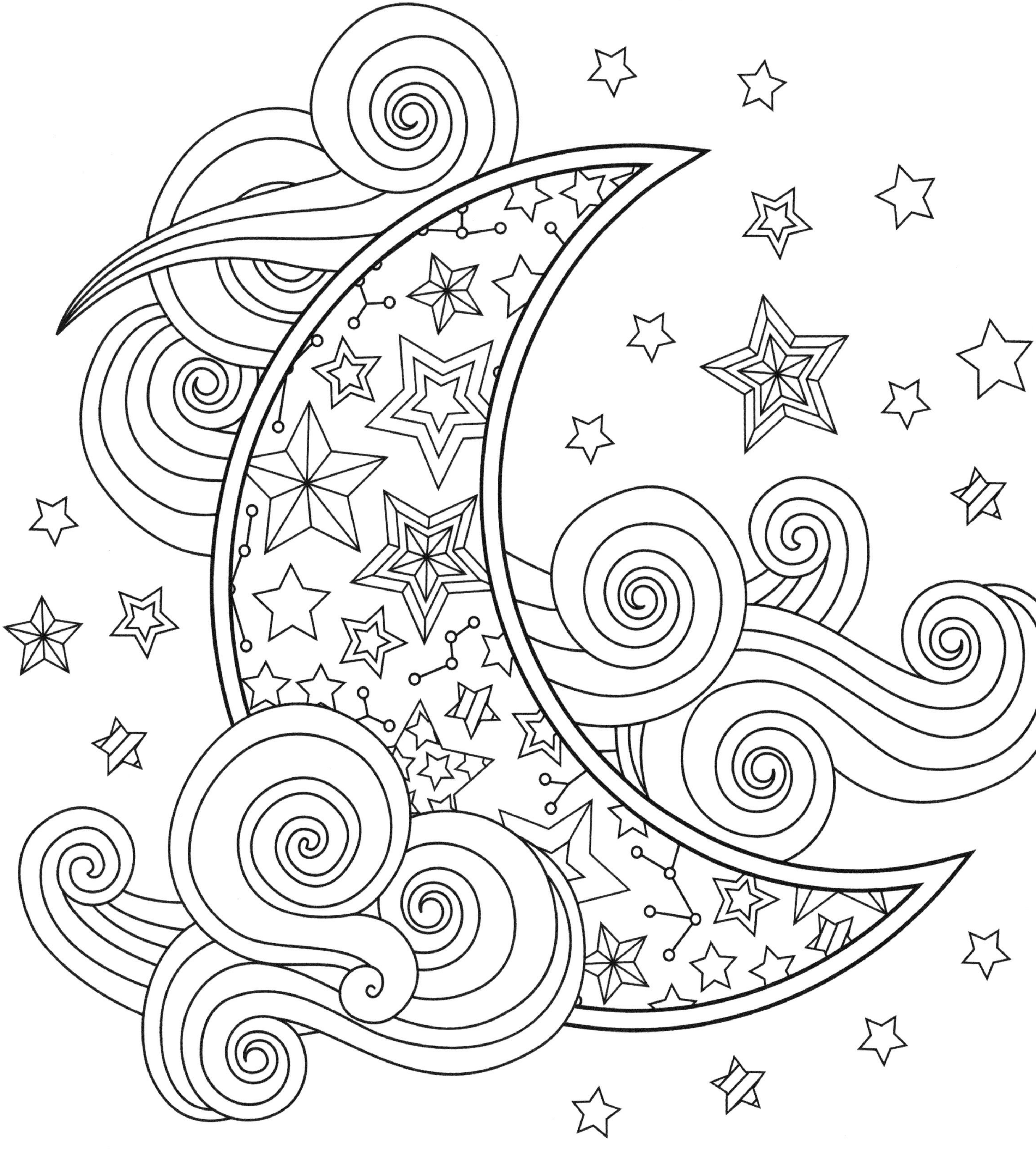

A Walk with Thelma

*The best reason for having dreams is that in
dreams no reasons are necessary.*
~Ashleigh Brilliant

"You look radiant," I squealed, locking my arm through Thelma's as we strolled down the cobblestone sidewalk. "Look at you. You don't seem ill at all – you positively glow!"

Like a couple of schoolgirls we giggled and caught up on the past few years. It felt incredible seeing Thelma again. Thelma was eighty-nine, decades ahead of me, but our age difference didn't matter. Our friendship had blossomed from the moment we set eyes on each other.

As we walked, I felt so relieved that Thelma appeared healthier than ever. "You know, Thelma," I said, "yesterday, I had the strongest feeling I should phone you."

Although the cozy little shops beckoned us, window-shopping could wait for another day. We were too enthralled, asking questions, and catching up with each other. The path that had seemed so long suddenly ended and we found ourselves standing alone before a green pasture.

"It's that time," Thelma announced.

After hugging, we clung to each other, our eyes full of tears. I wanted to hold her forever. "I know you know, that even though I don't call as often as I should, I love and miss you a lot," I said, embracing her once more.

"I do know you love me," Thelma answered softly. "I love you too."

"We've got to do this more often," I cried. "I promise I'll come see you soon."

I'll never forget the love on Thelma's face. Her expression reminded me what I already knew in my heart, that there wasn't going to be another visit with her. Thelma's misty eyes gleamed as she grabbed my hand one last time and then gently let go as she faded away into the light.

And in that instant I woke up, brushing the tears from my face, knowing that I would never see Thelma again because I had received a call from her son, earlier that same morning, informing me that Thelma had passed away.

Upon hearing of Thelma's death, a feverish guilt consumed me all day. If only I'd followed through with visits or heeded my gut and called her the day before she died. "There's always tomorrow," I assured myself, but Thelma's tomorrows had run out and I hadn't even said goodbye. When I needed her most, Thelma's love reached me in my dream so that I could try and move past my guilt.

–Jill Burns–

"I had the strongest feeling I should phone you."

"Look," she said, in that practical, knowing tone of hers that never failed to steady me. "I will always be near. Always. If after I'm gone there is a way, any way possible, I promise I'll let you know I'm around and watching over you." Then she would flick a hand and change the subject, as if to put the matter to rest.

Excerpt from "Mom Found a Way" by Paula L. Silici, a story in *Chicken Soup for the Soul: Angels & Miracles*

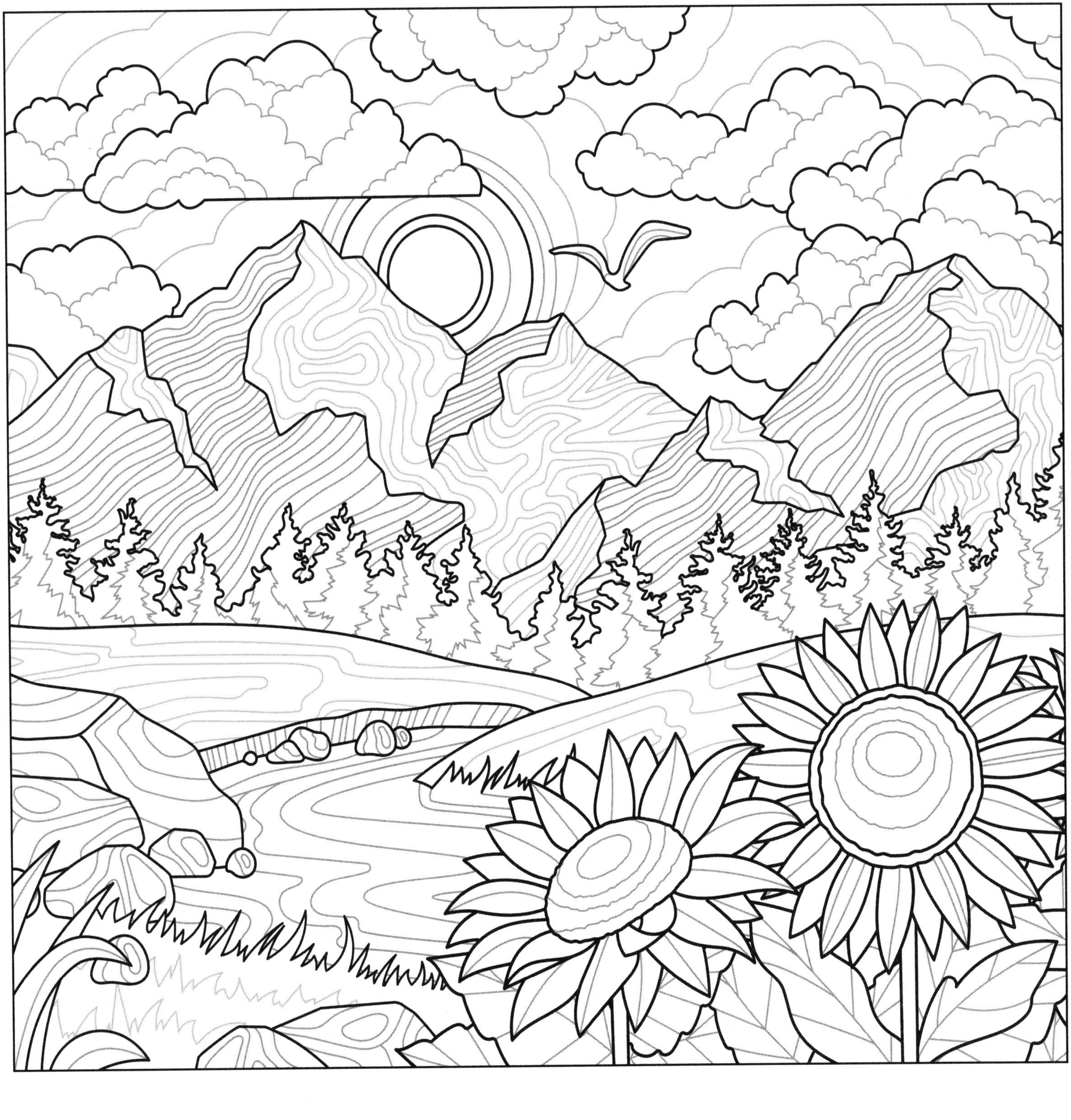

I Get Misty

A song will outlive all sermons in the memory.
~Henry Giles

My grandmother loved music and played the piano and the organ, and my mother played the piano as well. But she needed the sheet music for everything she played except for the song "Misty," which she knew by heart. It was a running joke in our family that every time we visited someone with a piano, at some point, my mother would sit down and laughingly ask, "Anybody wanna hear 'Misty'?"

My parents were married for forty-three years, taking up the RV lifestyle in their mid-fifties and traveling around the country. They settled in Longview, Texas, and bought a small house there. One night, my mother began to feel ill. She'd been plagued with respiratory problems most of her later life, and my father took her to the hospital. She was admitted for the night. The next morning, as my father was preparing to leave to visit her, the hospital called to tell him that my mother had passed away.

My father was shattered. I booked the next flight to Dallas, rented a car and headed to Longview.

Later that evening, I suggested we go out to dinner, if for no other reason than to get out of the house. He agreed, and off we went.

From the subdivision where my parents lived to the "restaurant row" of Longview was about a ten-minute drive. We ate dinner and tried to make conversation with each other. As we got in the car, I told my father that I wanted to make a stop at a convenience store to grab some diet soda. On the drive back, we began discussing the various things we needed to get done as far as a service, notifying out-of-town relatives, and other arrangements. As we talked and drove, I passed at least five or six different convenience stores, telling myself, "I'll stop at the next one."

Finally I came to an intersection that was also the turn-off to get to their subdivision. There was a store there, so I pulled in and got out, realizing that this was my last opportunity to grab some soda.

I opened the door and walked in, and as I did, I heard music coming from a radio behind the counter.

It was Johnny Mathis singing "Misty."

I froze. And then I smiled, realizing that it was my mother reaching out to me one more time, asking if I wanted to hear "Misty."

—Greg Moore—

Pennies from Paula

A strong friendship doesn't need daily conversation or being together.
As long as the relationship lives in the heart, true friends never part.
~Author Unknown

When my best friend, Paula, passed away eight years ago, my daughter had a difficult time working through the loss. McKenna was ten years old at the time and Paula was like a fun aunt to her. She would see or hear from Paula at least a couple of times a week. Paula was my backup sitter and a true comfort to McKenna when I was going through my divorce.

When Paula went into the hospital for her second transplant in 2007, I really did believe that she would sail through the procedure just like she had before. There was nothing in Paula's history with the disease that would make me believe anything different. She had been a fighter and a survivor since the day that she was first diagnosed with cancer.

When I realized that Paula would not be coming home from the hospital, I tried to prepare McKenna as best I could. My daughter had already experienced great loss when my grandmother passed away. But as McKenna reminded me, GG, short for Great-Grandma was older and that was what happened when people got old. Paula, on the other hand was not old, so death should not have been a possibility.

Telling McKenna that Paula had died was one of the hardest things I have ever done. There were tears, yelling and lots of sleepless nights. McKenna was afraid that if Paula could die young, so could I. I did my best to assure her that was not going to happen, but I know that she did not fully believe me. We prayed a lot.

During this time, I tried to keep McKenna busy so there would be less time to worry. I had her enter an art competition at my work. Students were asked to make something out of a generic, small box. McKenna decided to make a wishing well. It was really quite cute and she added pennies as part of the décor. When explaining her thoughts behind her "box art" creation, McKenna remembered what I had told her about finding pennies. I had told her it meant that someone in heaven was thinking about you. Her wishing well was actually a tribute to her friend Paula.

This simple piece of art seemed to do the trick. McKenna was feeling better and we were finding pennies everywhere… inside the house, the car, on walks, in parking lots, her room, my office, etc.

Then one night, when I was having a hard time falling asleep, I felt a presence in my room. I remember this feeling of peace and a swirling light hovering at the door. I was not frightened and I immediately knew that it was Paula.

The next morning when I woke up, before I could say anything about last night's "visit," my husband Joe said to me, "Paula was here last night." I asked him why he thought that. Joe is blind so I was pretty sure that he did not see the same light that I did. He then said that when he got up to go to the bathroom, he passed her in the doorway. He said that he felt a presence as he was walking by and immediately knew that it was Paula.

Needless to say, I was a little surprised when Joe shared his encounter with me. However, when I got out of bed and headed out of the room, I found a penny on the floor right where I saw the light. I knew that my dear friend had indeed stopped by.

—Laura Dailey-Pelle—

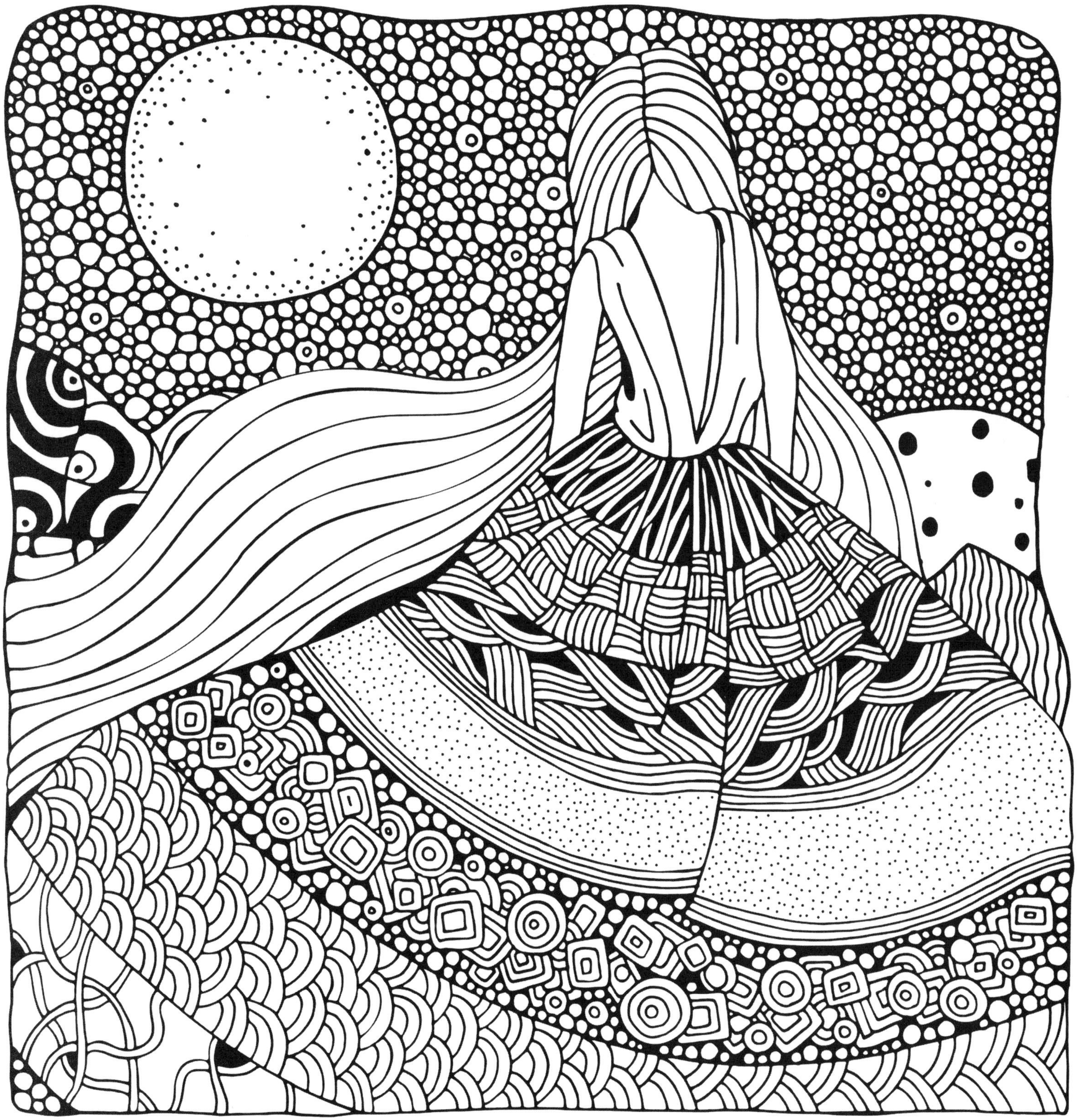

By a Hair

Love is the one thing we're capable of perceiving
that transcends dimensions of time and space.
~Interstellar

One weekday morning I pulled into the Great Clips parking lot for my normal quarter-inch trim. Then I looked in the rearview mirror and started second-guessing myself. Did I really need a haircut? I had driven fifteen minutes to get there and I don't know why I suddenly questioned my plan.

After staring into the mirror for a long time, I opted not to go inside. I would go pick up a prescription instead, at the pharmacy twenty blocks due north of Great Clips, on the same street in fact.

But then, I made my second unexplained decision of the morning; I started to drive east, back toward home, instead of up the road toward the pharmacy.

When I realized I was heading in the wrong direction, I decided to turn at the next intersection and head north. But then, for some reason I don't understand, I started zigzagging through the streets, not taking a direct route to the pharmacy. I felt like something was tugging at me now.

As I worked my way haphazardly toward the pharmacy, I came upon a sizeable traffic jam. It looked like it might be a wreck of some sort. I spotted a small street that would lead me around the slowdown and put me back on course in no time. The other drivers were taking the same detour, and as I began to follow them, I felt another tug, to get back in the traffic jam and head straight toward the wreck.

When I finally got to the accident that was causing the traffic jam, I saw a damaged white Acura SUV on the side of the road, right next to a police car and people milling about. My daughter Lauren had a car just like that. But it wouldn't be her – nothing bad could happen to my Lauren – the star athlete, tough dynamic mother of two little kids.

And then I saw her. It was Lauren. I parked across the street and walked over as casually as I could so as not to startle her. She was as stunned as I was. She had cuts and burns from the airbag but was displaying her legendary athletic toughness to be strong for her kids.

Thankfully they were solidly restrained in car seats and not hurt. I held three-year-old Ava while Lauren talked to the police. Ava wondered aloud why her car was so "dirty!" Little baby Drew was unaware of the upset, now dozing in his mother's arms.

Lauren kept asking me, "Why are you here?" I started to explain my haircut plans and my weird driving route but felt the whole story was too complicated and unbelievable. So I said, "I just thought you might need my help." As soon as I spoke I asked myself if that made sense. Did she understand what I meant? I later found out that she did.

My no-haircut day was over a year ago. I have often wondered how my meandering drive could lead me right to the crumpled SUV. I'm still puzzled why I didn't get that haircut in the first place.

– Doug Couch–

"I just thought you might need my help."

Meet The Contributors

The stories in this book were originally published in 2016, and these bios were current at the time of the original publication.

Monica A. Andermann lives and writes on Long Island where she shares a home with her husband and their little tabby Samson. Her writing has been included in such publications as *Woman's World, Sasee* and *Guideposts* as well as many *Chicken Soup for the Soul* books.

Peggy Archer is the author of picture books for children, including *Turkey Surprise*, a *New York Times* bestseller. Besides writing, she enjoys walking, line dancing, and time with her grandchildren. She and her husband have six children and eleven grandchildren. They live in O'Fallon, MO. Visit her at peggyarcher.com.

Lainie Belcastro has many titles in the arts, but her most treasured title is mom to her daughter Nika. Together they created the trademarked storytellers, Mrs. Terra Cotta Pots & Twig, who plant dreams for children! Lainie, a published writer, has signed with a children's book publisher. She plans to live "happily ever after!"

Lily Blais works in risk analysis but writing is her passion. Her first novel is complete and she is currently submitting it to literary agencies. Time with family and friends means the world to her and she has just welcomed into the world her first grandchild.

Jill Burns lives in the mountains of West Virginia with her wonderful family. She's a retired piano teacher and performer. She enjoys writing, music, gardening, nature, and spending time with her grandchildren.

Sharon Carpenter earned her B.A. degree in History and English at Jacksonville State University, and her M.A. degree from the University of Memphis. She teaches middle schoolers in Memphis and tries to avoid Elvis Week. Her biggest fans are her husband Jesse and three incredible kids who turned into amazing adults.

Pastor Wanda Christy-Shaner runs a Facebook page called "Good News Only," a site developed for prayer and praise. She has been previously published in the *Chicken Soup for the Soul* series, as well as *War Cry*. She is an award-winning speaker, actress and adrenaline junkie. E-mail her at seekingtruth65@yahoo.com.

Doug Couch earned an Ed.D from The University of Kansas and retired from the University of Central Missouri as Director of Academic Advising. He and his wife, Peggy, have four children and twelve grandchildren. Doug passed away in October 2015, and this piece demonstrates that his greatest joy was his family.

Mike D'Alto received his Master's of Creative Writing degree from Queens College in 2013 and a Bachelor of Arts degree from Hofstra University in 2007. He teaches English at Suffolk Community College and tutors high school students for standardized tests. He enjoys writing poetry and one-act plays.

Laura Dailey-Pelle received her master's degree in Health Care Administration from Central Michigan University. She works at a hospital in southeast Michigan as Director of Radiation Oncology and Healing Arts. Laura enjoys walking, reading, writing, photography and spending time with her family.

Grace Givens has only recently begun writing about the many serendipitous occurrences in her life. A veteran performer, she is a cancer survivor who sings through her exams, tests and treatments. She and her husband Robert reside in Houston, TX. E-mail her at gracegivens@gmail.com or view her at youtube/gracegivens/survive.

Pebbles H. writes leisurely on her personal blog at pebblesinthesun.wordpress.com and professionally as a marketer. Armed with an over-imaginative mind and her love of languages, Pebbles hopes to publish her poetry collection and write children's books that will inspire all.

Judith Ann Hayes loves to write! She is an avid reader. Her older daughter is a registered nurse and her younger daughter is a make-up artist; both are happily married. Judith is a very proud grandmother. She loves to spend time with